BARYSHNIKOV IN RUSSIA

TEXT AND PHOTOGRAPHS BY

NINA ALOVERT

TRANSLATED BY IRENE HUNTOON

HOLT, RINEHART
AND WINSTON
NEW YORK

T O   F R I E N D S
I N   L E N I N G R A D

Library of Congress Cataloging in Publication Data
Alovert, Nina.
Baryshnikov in Russia.
Includes bibliographical references.
1. Baryshnikov, Mikhail, 1948–   .   2. Ballet
dancers—Russian S.F.S.R.—Biography.   3. Russian
S.F.S.R.—Social conditions.   I. Title.
GV1785.B348A76   1984   792.8'2'0924 [B]   83-13012
ISBN: 0-03-062589-0

F I R S T   E D I T I O N

Design by Amy Hill
Printed in the United States of America
1   3   5   7   9   10   8   6   4   2

•   •   •

FRONTISPIECE: *Baryshnikov as Albrecht in a 1972*
Soviet television production of Petipa's Giselle.

ISBN 0-03-062589-0

CONTENTS

TRANSLATOR'S NOTE

In this translation from the Russian, the proper names of people still living in the Soviet Union have been transliterated according to the system of the United States Board on Geographic Names, which is recommended in the Chicago Manual of Style. I have, however, substituted a "y" for an "iy" ending.

In cases where Russian names are well known in an alternate form to English-speaking audiences, the conventional spellings have been retained.

Further, the names of Russians now living in the West have been spelled in the manner in which each individual has transliterated his own name.

PREFACE

Mikhail Baryshnikov has had the opportunity of living two lives in the course of one. He has his life in America still before him, but his life in Russia is over—and about that life it is possible to write with finality. I knew Baryshnikov in his Russian life and saw him onstage at the Kirov Theater in Leningrad, from his first appearance as a graduate of the ballet school to his last performance there.

I had almost finished writing a doctoral dissertation in history at Leningrad State University when I received an irresistible invitation to work at the Theater of Comedy. Abandoning my graduate studies of the early-fifteenth-century artisans of the city of Lübeck, I became manager of the museum at the theater under the direction of the remarkable Nikolai Akimov. There I fell in love with the stage and, from 1974 to 1977 (the year I left for the West), I worked as a professional photographer in Leningrad's dramatic theaters.

Years before, I had begun photographing ballet, because of my love for this art form. I began to publish ballet photographs in magazines, newspapers, and books in 1961. From that time I was always given official permission to shoot in the theater during performances.

Because of my work and my acquaintance with many critics, directors, actors, and dancers, including Mikhail Baryshnikov, I was familiar with the problems of backstage life in Leningrad's theaters.

This book is not a critical analysis of Baryshnikov's art, nor is it a biography of the man. It is my reminiscences of my friend Mikhail Baryshnikov, in words and photographs, as I knew him in Leningrad. I have tried to reproduce the atmosphere and emotions of that time exactly as we lived then.

As a matter of principle, I photographed ballets during performances, despite all of the technical difficulties. It is less important to me to create an "artistic" photograph than to preserve the moment of creativity onstage, which not even the most brilliant artist can reproduce in a studio. Dance is dearer to me than the art of photography.

When I left the Soviet Union, I was unable to carry my own negatives with me, since it is against Soviet law to take negatives out of the country. I had to send the negatives with foreigners, who are not always searched at customs. It was necessary to pack the negatives tightly so that they occupied as little space as possible. In one case an American acquaintance carried some of my negatives out tucked in her boots. Not surprisingly, in the course of being shipped in far less than ideal circumstances, the emulsion on the film deteriorated and many of the negatives became scratched. Nevertheless, because of the uniqueness of these photographs of Baryshnikov's Russian career, we have decided to publish some of the pictures despite their poor condition.

I hope readers will indulge my recital of stories about Baryshnikov in which I figure. I include these as characteristic of ordinary Soviet life, which Baryshnikov also lived. Sadly, I was unable to write about most of Baryshnikov's friends, because they are still living in Leningard. The names of those who are mentioned have been changed. Someday, perhaps, both Russian ballet critics and Misha's friends will be able to discuss openly this outstanding Russian dancer, possibly in more detail and more interestingly than I have succeeded in doing.

Nina Alovert

ACKNOWLEDGMENTS

hen we arrive in the West, we Russians find ourselves having to start anew, from zero. I want to express my deepest gratitude to all the people who have helped me in my new life to publish my book on Mikhail Baryshnikov.

The idea of publishing a collection of my photographs in the West occurred to me after Baryshnikov defected, but to do so in Russia became impossible. This book would never have been written had I not had the good fortune of meeting, through my friends Eugene Belokon and Vicente Garcia Marquez, Parmenia Migel Ekstrom, a writer and connoisseur of ballet and an organizer of the Stravinsky-Diaghilev Foundation. Mrs. Ekstrom took an interest in my photographs, supported my idea of a book on Baryshnikov in Leningrad, and introduced me to Donald Hutter, then editor in chief at Holt, Rinehart and Winston.

I consider myself fortunate in having worked both with Mr. Hutter and with Jennifer Josephy, who took over the project. The period when I worked with them on my book was the happiest time I have had in America.

I want to thank Mikhail Baryshnikov for correcting my mistakes when reading the manuscript and for providing details that I did not remember. I am grateful to my translator, Irene Huntoon, who with unfailing patience and a sense of humor worked on endless drafts. I also wish to thank Elena Gorokhova and Alexander Sumerkin, who translated some small additions to the text after Irene Huntoon had completed her translation. Also, I want to use this occasion to thank my friends Eva Hirsch and Leonid Lubianitsky who, from the moment we met in the United States, supported my idea of publishing my photographs of Baryshnikov. I am indebted to Alexander Minz, Slava Santnaneev, Kira Zherzhevskaya, and Bella Kovarskaya, as well as many others, who helped me reconstruct the chronology of events and the list of roles Baryshnikov performed in Russia. I am particularly grateful to the photographer, who must remain anonymous, who sent me copies of photographs that I had left in Russia.

I want to thank publicly the first readers of my Russian manuscript: my mother, Elena Tudorovskaya, who is also a professional literary critic, and art designer Zoya Lymar-Krasnovsky, who graduated from the Leningrad ballet school the same year as Mikhail Baryshnikov. Their comments helped me improve the Russian text of the book. And I want to thank my son, Igor Alovert, and my friend Elena Levina for helping me understand the English translation.

I owe a debt of gratitude to various editors of New York–based Russian periodicals who published my articles on ballet, which were to become the basis of the present book: Alex Batchan, Sergei Dovlatov, Mikhail Morgulis, Andrei Sedykh, as well as Vladimir Maramzin, an editor of the Russian magazine *Echo*, published in Paris.

And, finally, my thanks go to all the friends who, each in his or her own way, helped and encouraged me in the process of working on the book: Nina Britto, Vladimir Gilman, Alexis Krasnovsky, Jonathan Lash, Herman J. Nadel, Natalya Sharymova, Andrei Perlstein, Deborah D. Mathews, Foundation CASE, and many others.

BARYSHNIKOV IN RUSSIA

ONE

THE DEFECTION

And all the same it's a pity that Baryshnikov is dancing in New York.

—from the anonymous contemporary Russian
song, "To All the Friends Who Have Left"

M isha Baryshnikov defected from the USSR while on tour in Canada, requesting political asylum from the American consulate in Toronto, on June 29, 1974. The evening of June 30, I attended the premiere of a new ballet, *Yaro-slavna*, at the Maly Opera Theater in Leningrad, choreographed by the young ballet master Oleg Vinogradov to the music of Boris Tishchenko.

In the overcrowded lobby of the theater, people greeted each other with the anxious question, "Why is Baryshnikov returning to Leningrad ahead of schedule?" Apparently, someone had remarked in an offhand manner, "Well, Baryshnikov will soon be back." But an acquaintance of Misha's and mine, Larisa, heard this comment and attached her own meaning to it. She greeted everyone entering the lobby by saying, "Have you heard? Baryshnikov is coming to see the premiere this evening!" Although the misunderstanding was soon cleared up, many patrons, while waiting for the performance to begin, continued to crane their necks to see whether Baryshnikov would actually enter the auditorium. Ironically, this irrational stir coincided with the moment at which Misha forever relinquished the possibility of entering the small, intimate, red-velvet

Group scene from the Maly Theater production of Yaroslavna. Choreographer: Oleg Vinogradov. This ballet had its premiere June 30, 1974, one day after Baryshnikov defected.

auditorium of the Maly Theater. However, Vinogradov's ballet soon occupied the minds and emotions of the audience. Baryshnikov was forgotten, until the morning of the following day.

On Monday, the first of July, my day was planned down to the last minute. But at eight o'clock in the morning, a friend called and said, "Now don't get scared, but just a minute ago the 'naughty voice' [Voice of America radio broadcast] announced that Misha Baryshnikov has disappeared."

The news stunned me. The notion that Misha had chosen to stay in the West did not occur to me immediately. All of our friends with whom I spoke that morning were also in a state of shock.

At eleven o'clock on that same morning, an unknown man telephoned and sternly informed me that he was calling from the KGB. (I was so agitated that afterward I did not remember his name or his rank.) He invited me to come to the KGB for a conversation. When I arrived at the KGB Leningrad headquarters that afternoon, I met a middle-aged man with straight, close-cropped hair, dressed in civilian clothing that had been stylish in the fifties; in short, he was just a simple Soviet citizen in a responsible position. He seemed slightly pained by the work at hand.

"Tell me, who called you this morning to tell you that Baryshnikov disappeared?" It was then that I realized that my telephone was being tapped by the KGB. Later, I became accustomed to this eavesdropping. The main question the investigator asked me was, "Did you know that Baryshnikov would stay abroad?"

"No," I answered quite truthfully. Indeed, I had had no idea. I was convinced that he had not planned in advance to defect.

"Well, then, write a letter to Baryshnikov."

Naturally, I categorically refused to write a letter. However, the discussion continued. "What, in your opinion, should I write to him?" I asked.

"Tell him that he should return."

"And to where? Directly to Siberia? To the Kirov Theater?" The official began to laugh. Even he realized that our conversation was more like vaudeville than a dramatic scene.

"What do you think? Who among Misha's friends was able to persuade him to remain abroad?"

I was astonished. The psychology of KGB workers sometimes leaves Soviet citizens at a loss. How does one make sense of such questions? Are they playing a game with us in order to have something to report back to their bosses, or do they themselves believe what they are saying? Later, knowledgeable people explained to me that apparently the KGB had earnestly sought to uncover a "conspiracy," particularly among the highly intellectual, nonconformist people in those literary and artistic circles in which Misha had close friends.

"Baryshnikov is a mature and independent person," I answered. "It is impossible to persuade him to do anything he does not choose to do."

"What, in general, do you think of him?" In response, I gave a eulogy, as if over the coffin of one deceased.

The official produced several sheets of white paper and a ball-point pen so that I would write this panegyric down. He left the room, leaving a young man in his place. Unlike his boss, the young man was very stylishly dressed in "imported" clothing; he even had on a tie with brown dots that matched the color of his eyes. But when the telephone rang,

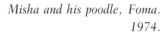

*Misha and his poodle, Foma.
1974.*

ABOVE RIGHT. *The apartment
building on the Moika Canal
where Baryshnikov lived during
1973–1974. It was the last
apartment he occupied in
Russia.* RIGHT. *Misha's friend
Slava Santnaneev and Misha's
teacher Aleksandr Pushkin, at
Pushkin's apartment. 1965.
(From the private collection of
Slava Santnaneev)*

the young man answered in military fashion, "Private Ivanov speaking!"

I had soon finished writing my glowing testimonial to Baryshnikov's virtues, but the official did not return for quite a while. Meanwhile, Private Ivanov engaged me in a discussion about ballet. He proved to be very well informed on this topic. We did not speak about Baryshnikov. Only once did Private Ivanov say something about his superior. "It's a bad break for him. He was supposed to start his vacation today and here it is, Monday, the first of July. With an affair like this, it doesn't look good. . . . Well, if something awful has happened to Baryshnikov, all right. But what if it's a defection?"

His callous remarks infuriated me, and I did not respond. Seeing that the conversation was at an end, Ivanov gave me some sort of magazine. I looked at it without seeing a word. From time to time, when I raised my eyes from the journal, I met a terrifying, unblinking gaze from a stone face. It is indeed possible to recognize KGB men by their look.

After about two hours the chief reappeared. He cheerfully entered the room, regarded me, and said, "You are quite calm, not the least bit agitated. You probably knew that Baryshnikov would stay!"

Completely frustrated, I asked, "Where does this leave me? What are you waiting for, for me to burst into tears right here?"

I did not know then that Larisa, on the other side of the wall, found herself practically sobbing, not from fear, but from her own feelings about Misha's disappearance. She agreed to write a letter to Misha. Later, Larisa told me all about her visit. To my amazed questioning as to why she had said yes to the KGB, she answered in a tragic tone, "I thought that perhaps I would never have the chance to write him another letter."

Larisa was the first person I had called on that morning after hearing that Misha had disappeared. A serious woman who taught Russian language and literature at one of Leningrad's colleges, she loved the ballet and understood it well. She lived by herself and was very much of a loner, for, although she was not without a sense of humor, her intolerance toward contrary opinions and her devotion to her own ideas scared most people away from close friendship with her. Larisa, however, idolized Misha. (There was probably not one ballet fan in all of Leningrad who did not.) Misha greatly valued her opinion of his performances but was rather afraid of her sharp tone and her aggressiveness in expressing her views.

I knew that the only way to avoid further contact with the KGB was to show complete obstinacy. I turned out to be right. After Larisa had broken down at the KGB, she received occasional visits from quiet, polite, young people who asked, each time, whether or not she'd heard anything about Misha; they suggested that she try persuading all of Misha's friends to write to him and advise him to return. Once, according to Larisa, she asked one of them, "Where would we be telling him to return to? To prison?"

"He would return to the theater."

"No one would believe that," Larisa retorted.

"But you believe me, don't you?"

Larisa, a very intelligent person, answered, "I believe you." In telling me this story, she added, "His eyes fluttered and he quietly said, 'Thank you.' " I couldn't believe it. A KGB agent quivering with emotion! The situation after Baryshnikov's defection was so nerve-racking, since it had been entirely unexpected, that many people, including Larisa, did not know what to think. She lost her head and even believed an agent of the KGB.

In general, Larisa was a brave woman. Later, after Misha reached me by telephone, she unhesitatingly requested that Misha call her also.

During my interview with the KGB, I was asked, as were all others, what could have persuaded Baryshnikov to remain in the West. I answered that the complete disintegration of the Kirov Theater and the lack of any creative work there was sufficient cause. "But, you know, we fired Konstantin Sergeyev, the artistic director, just a few years ago," the officer replied with some surprise. Most of Misha's friends who were called to the KGB and who told me about their visits gave approximately the same answers. One tried to respond to all of the questions with, "I don't know."

Slowly, my conversation with the official drew to a close. "So, you won't write a letter?"

"No."

"If you find anything out about Baryshnikov . . ."

"What could I possibly hear about him before you?"

"Well, if you hear anything, let us know. I will give you my telephone number if you like."

"No, I don't want it."

Having ended the interview, the officer escorted me to the exit from the KGB headquarters. While descending the staircase with me, he suddenly dropped the official jargon and asked in a natural tone of voice, "Tell me—it's true, isn't it, that he had a good apartment?"

I thought to myself that perhaps these people are so accustomed to selling their own fathers for promotion in the service and for other material rewards that they cannot understand how nonmaterial considerations can motivate others.

The investigation into Misha's disappearance continued for two or three more days. After it was completed, everything quieted down and Baryshnikov was almost forgotten. Almost. Soon, by one means, then another, various idiotic stories about Baryshnikov surfaced. The OBKhSS (the Department of Battle Against the Embezzlement of Socialist Property and Speculation) tried to seize Misha's car from the person with whom he had left it for safekeeping. Next, the army suddenly began drafting boys from the Kirov Ballet. (Despite the compulsory military service throughout the Soviet Union, ballet dancers are usually exempted, since the interruption in their dancing for two to three years would effectively end their careers.) One obtuse military officer, when asked by the boys why he showed such zeal, blurted out, "You won't be running off like Baryshnikov!" As the story received a lot of publicity, the boys were soon returned to the theater.

After my visit to the KGB, my telephone remained connected to its office for another two or three days. On the day following my visit, a friend who had come to see me suggested calling for the time. I picked up the receiver and dialed the number, but all I heard at the other end was a sepulchral silence. We all knew that if a telephone is tied to the KGB for eavesdropping, it is impossible to call services with recorded messages, such as the time or weather. "No," I said to my friend, "there is no time for you today."

"What scoundrels," she joked. "Because of them it would be impossible to call an ambulance."

As we continued to chat, I sat holding the receiver. "Since it's impossible to dial the time," I remarked, "they ought to tell us instead." At that, a giggling male voice resounded from the receiver, "Two minutes after twelve."

Two days later, I went with Asya, one of Misha's friends, to see what was happening in Misha's apartment. Asya had begun frequenting Misha's home not long before his departure. Once, after we had both spent an evening at Misha's, she called me and asked in an agitated voice, "Didn't you notice anything? It seems to me that Misha is interested in me!" Asya was a typical "Petersburg girl," brought up on nineteenth-century Russian literature, who was susceptible to romantic self-deception. We were not able to ascertain the truth of Asya's observations because Misha left for Canada soon after that. But the game of Asya's romance with Baryshnikov continued. It consisted in my telling fortunes to Asya with a deck of cards. It turned out that the King of Diamonds was thinking of the dark-eyed Asya every day and was yearning for her with all his heart, from stiflingly hot Canada. As for Asya, still in Leningrad, "I don't like the curtains on his windows, they're too gloomy," she said pensively. "I will hang silver ones." When Misha defected, Asya felt and acted almost like a widow.

Misha's last apartment in Leningrad was in an attractive building that had been a nobleman's private residence prior to the 1917 revolution. It was located on the Moika Canal, not far from the Winter Palace. The apartment had high ceilings and large windows, but these were practically its only pleasant features. Apartments that had been created by subdividing former private residences barely met the demands of modern comfort. Misha's apartment was located on the sixth floor. There was no elevator in the building and the staircase, which was unlighted, was incredibly steep (formerly called a "black" staircase, it had been for the use of servants). One had to find the apartment intuitively.

In the apartment itself, there was hot water only in the kitchen, which also served as an entrance hall. The kitchen led into the spacious dining room, where Misha had put his television (a color set, a luxury at that time), a large expandable dining table, a sideboard for the dishes, and a comfortable leather armchair. There were two doors at the far side of the dining room. One opened into a tiny room where Misha kept his rather large library. The other led into the bedroom, which had an

ABOVE LEFT. *Alexander Minz as Hans in* Giselle. *Petrozavodsk. 1960–1961.*

ABOVE. *Natalia Yudeleva and Alexander Minz in the Spanish Dance from* Swan Lake. *Kirov Theater. 1967–1968.*

alcove. The windows of the apartment looked out into the courtyard. From the bedroom one entered the bathroom. The bathroom had no hot running water; it was necessary to light a wood fire in the stove underneath a tank of water before taking a shower.

Slava Santnaneev opened the door for us. Slava is a geologist by profession. His friendship with Misha began in the spring of 1967. They met at the home of the remarkable teacher of classical dance, Aleksandr Pushkin, with whom Slava had long been friendly. Slava was, and still is—he now lives in the West—one of the oldest and one of the closest of Misha's friends. Their relationship developed into a familial one long ago. In Leningrad, Slava had lived in Misha's apartment when he left on long trips. Therefore, I was not surprised when Slava greeted us.

At the door, he said in a whisper, "Be careful, there is a *stukach* in the apartment." (*Stukach* is a slang expression for a person who is not directly employed by the KGB but serves as an informant, "knocking," or reporting, on people.) I guessed immediately who it was as I entered the room. At that instant, all of my conjectures about one of Misha's friends hardened into certainty.

I walked through the kitchen and into the dining room. There, in

9

the evening light, the gloomy Suslik was sitting right on the dining-room table.

Suslik (the Russian word for "gopher") was a nickname acquired at college; it suited the man so well that it replaced his last name. Suslik had met Misha within the Leningrad theater circles that he frequented, although he was not professionally involved in theater. He had become particularly friendly with Misha during the last season, 1973–1974, and was a constant companion. Misha, just before his departure, had apparently begun to feel a little oppressed by Suslik's continual presence. After Misha defected, there was a joke in Leningrad that he was running away from Suslik; there was no other way to shake him off. When it became known that Misha had remained in the West, Suslik was away from Leningrad on an official business trip. A colleague, who was traveling with him, told me that Suslik heard the news on board a plane en route to Leningrad, when co-workers who did not like him gloatingly informed him of the staggering event. Suslik drank vodka throughout the remainder of the flight. After landing, he did not go home, where he assumed that an invitation for him to appear promptly at the KGB was waiting. He rushed from the airport directly to the home of some of Misha's friends. Arriving there, he literally crawled underneath a bed and groaned continually, "They are going to get me by the balls now!" In general, he behaved very strangely that day. These and other stories had flooded back into my head at Slava's whispered warning. Later, other evidence confirmed our assumption. From the authorities' point of view, it was absolutely necessary to place an informer near a leading dancer, a *vyezdnoi* or "leaving" person who is included in foreign tours. It is possible that this was Suslik's assignment. Despite this, he could have sincerely loved Misha. One circumstance does not preclude the other.

Suslik was detained no longer than anyone else at the KGB. But what they discussed with him, he did not say.

I entered the dining room, greeted the morose Suslik, and walked about Misha's "dead" apartment. When I returned to the kitchen, Slava begged for help. "Get him out of here on some sort of pretext. He sits here all day long, every day."

I reentered the dining room and asked Suslik to walk Asya and me to the trolleybus. To my amazement, he gladly agreed to go. But what a

FACING PAGE. *Minz as Drosselmeyer in Baryshnikov's production of* The Nutcracker. *American Ballet Theatre. 1978.*

11

cheerless stroll it was! Tragically silent Asya. Irascible Suslik. And I was certainly not in the mood for light and sociable conversation. Amid the splendor of the gray-green light that illuminates Leningrad during the white nights of summer, we were crossing the Palace Bridge, in one of the most beautiful spots in the city, when Suslik suddenly stopped. "Well, tell me," he demanded. "What did Slava say to you? Did he say something about me? Well, what did he say? Tell me!" It seemed to me that he might push me off the bridge in his agitation. I feigned surprise.

Afterward, I felt sorry for Suslik when many of his acquaintances shunned him. He must have felt like a pariah. I realized that, regardless of my feelings, he had been Misha's friend; furthermore, I did not have the right to judge him sternly, as I did not have unassailable proof of his guilt. We later met from time to time. But I remember him most clearly on the Palace Bridge, one of Misha's closest friends looking at me with the face of a hunted animal.

I did not return to Misha's apartment again.

Soon, we had heard over the Voice of America that Misha was in New York, had danced *Giselle* with the American Ballet Theatre, and had received tremendous acclaim. I managed to contact Misha through Alexander ("Sasha") Minz, a principal dancer with ABT at that time. Minz had been a friend of Baryshnikov's in Leningrad. He emigrated some time earlier.

When the troupe of Soviet artists flew to Canada, Sasha traveled to Toronto especially to see Misha. Misha spent all of his free time in Toronto with Sasha. During the Soviet troupe's appearances in Toronto, the two discussed the possibilities of Baryshnikov's working in the West. After Misha's defection, Sasha gave Misha moral support throughout the most difficult period of his acclimatization to America. Sasha, who has a heart of gold, radiates infinite kindness toward all of the people around him, especially his friends.

Minz graduated as a character dancer from the Leningrad Vaganova Institute in 1960. While still in school, Sasha danced roles that demanded acting capabilities from the performer. But he was not accepted into the Kirov Theater at that time, for reasons which no one could understand. While Sasha was still in school, the leading Russian ballet critic Yury Slonimsky had noticed his talent. Minz worked for two years in the theater of opera and ballet in the beautiful northern city of Petrozavodsk. There he danced the principal character roles. I had been friendly with Minz for a long time and often went to see him perform. He was young and touchingly in love as Hans in *Giselle* and romantic as Espada in *Don Quixote*. After two years, Minz returned to Leningrad, to the Kirov Theater, where he danced in the *corps de ballet*. From time to time he performed solo character dances, but he was not given any interesting roles. Not once did he receive a part in which he could reveal his unconventional artistic talent. Minz began to fulfill his potential only after he came to America.

While still in Leningrad, I heard about the critical acclaim that Minz received as Drosselmeyer in the *Nutcracker* staged by Baryshnikov. When Misha called me soon after the premiere, I said, "All of Sasha's friends are grateful to you for giving him an important role in your ballet."

"What do you mean?!" Misha answered. "It is I who am grateful to Sasha: he made my ballet a success."

And so, thanks to Sasha, I got in touch with Misha. I had sent a telegram to Sasha because I was not sure that one addressed directly to Misha would be allowed through the border. At this time Sasha's mother was ill; therefore I wrote, "Worried about mother's health. Call immediately."

A week went by. I sat at home, almost never going out. But Sasha did not call. After a week, a friend of his in Leningrad called me and said, "Where have you been lately? Sasha called me and complained that he hasn't been able to reach you. The operator keeps saying, 'The telephone is ringing; there's no one at home.' "

This is an ordinary device of the KGB. Since, in the Soviet Union, there is no direct telephone connection with America, calls are placed through an operator. If a telephone conversation is not allowed, the Western party is told that there is no answer.

After learning that Sasha had received my first telegram, I immediately sent a second one: "Sitting at home, waiting for call." I became rooted to my apartment. Several days went by. Finally my telephone rang unexpectedly at four o'clock one morning.

"32-88-17? New York is calling."

It seemed to me that I waited a long time for the conversation to   *13* begin. I was barefoot, as I had leapt up out of bed to answer the telephone and stood shivering on the cold floor of the hallway. Pressing the receiver against my ear, I listened to the sounds of another civilization. The operators conversed in an unfamiliar language. In the rustling of the global ether, I tried to detect the first sounds of Sasha's voice. But then the breathing of the other world stopped; the operator said, "Speak!" In the ensuing quiet I heard Sasha's voice so distinctly it was as if he were calling from the neighboring apartment.

"Is everything all right with you?" Sasha asked carefully.

"Do you see Misha?"

"Yes, of course."

I had one aim: to let Misha know that we did not betray him and still loved him as before. "Tell him," I said loudly and deliberately, "that I will always remember him as one of the most remarkable, noble, and worthy people who has ever lived."

"Wait a minute," said Sasha somewhat hesitatingly. For some time the receiver was silent.

It did not occur to me that Misha was sitting right there, next to the telephone. Therefore, when I heard Misha's voice quietly gasping with emotion, I lost my head completely and shouted into the receiver, "Minechka! Just don't hang up!" Why did I think that he would hang up? Who can predict what sort of nonsense we will utter in a moment of sudden, heartfelt emotion?

Thus began the "telephone vigils" and "telephone guests." Misha usually called either Larisa or myself on his and our birthdays. On these occasions, those of Misha's friends who could not speak with him on their own telephone because they were afraid or worked in restricted fields, or lived in communal apartments, gathered at Larisa's or my apartment.

During the first years in America, Misha suffered dreadfully over the separation from his friends. We listened painstakingly to Misha's voice during short and disjointed conversations. Heeding the squeak of the recording devices and practically hearing the breathing of the operators who were listening to us, we attempted to say something meaningful about love and inevitable reunions. We tried to read his mood from his intonation.

FACING PAGE. *Misha in his apartment on the Moika Canal. 1974.*

14

With the passage of time the affection of Leningrad's inhabitants for Misha did not diminish. Not only close friends or acquaintances, but also people who had only seen him onstage, continued to think and talk about him. I remember one funny episode involving Misha's dog, Foma, an enormous, white, standard poodle, still living in Leningrad to this day. Not long after Misha's defection, the woman with whom Foma now lives entered him in a dog show. The name of the owner, Baryshnikov, still remained in Foma's pedigree papers. No one knew what reaction the judges would have to this situation. But the principal judge, when awarding Foma the gold medal, declared, "We will not hurt the feelings of Baryshnikov's dog."

We all listened to the Voice of America and passed on the news about Misha. The KGB, in its own way, tried to counter this love and admiration. In an effort to neutralize the scandal, they started rumors that Baryshnikov had simply received permission to dance abroad for two years, for the development of his individuality and for the glory of Soviet art. After that, gossip spread that Misha was unhappy, that he repented of his foolishness, that he was literally living on the steps of the Soviet Embassy in Washington and begging that he be allowed to return. Since I had some contact with Misha himself and had heard about his life through other sources as well, I took exception with a vengeance to the routine fabrications of the KGB that people repeated to me.

But, after a while, the rumors began to trouble all of Misha's friends and admirers. What if there were some truth to these stories? We secured a meeting with a highly placed government official and asked him in private, "What would happen if Baryshnikov were to return?"

With knitted brows, the official paused for a long moment and finally said, "Tell him that he should never return."

We described this and other incidents to Misha through unofficial channels. Misha called me and said, "I received all of your letters; don't worry about me. I am not planning to do anything foolish."

Misha's defection had stunned many people. Some who had been unquestioningly struggling along with their everyday troubles up until that time suddenly stopped to wonder, "What is going on if people as celebrated, as well-to-do, and as loved by all as Misha run away from the country?" The love for Misha and for his art, which had been one of the only rays of light in many lives, was so great that there were people who decided to leave Russia themselves after Misha's flight.

There was no doubt in anyone's mind that Misha, as an artist, had done the right thing for himself. This comforted those who were left behind. We knew that he would remember his friends, even at the height of his fame in the West, and that he would yearn for his early years at the Kirov Theater.

Since his defection, Misha's image has lost much of its reality for many in Leningrad. To some extent Misha has been turned into a symbol of freedom, of success, and of sublime art. There is a song by the famous Russian *chansonnier* and poet Bulat Okudzhava that was applied to Misha after he left:

> *Mozart plays on an antique violin,*
> *Mozart plays and the violin sings.*
> *Mozart his country he did not choose,*
> *He just plays his whole life through.*

THE EARLY YEARS

It is truly an enigmatic concept—what is talent?

—Nikolai Akimov, *Theatrical Heritage*

M | ikhail Nikolaevich Baryshnikov was born in the city of Riga, Latvia, on January 27, 1948. He first studied ballet at the Riga Choreographic Institute and then at the Agrippina Vaganova Choreographic Institute under the tutelage of Aleksandr Pushkin. He graduated in 1967. I did not know Baryshnikov during his student years, nor did I see him in his first performance in Leningrad when the Latvian ballet company toured in 1964 and Baryshnikov danced the solo of the Young Boy with the Bow in the ballet *Shanutala*. I do remember conversations among balletomanes at that time about an outstanding pupil at the Riga Institute. Later, Alexander Minz, a dancer with the Kirov Ballet at the time, described Misha's first appearance in Leningrad. Sasha said that he was startled not only by the technical perfection and artistry of this young boy but also by the fact that he already had the stage presence of a mature soloist.

The Leningrad television studio filmed Baryshnikov during the Latvian company's tour. The television editor, Boris Tolchinsky, asked Leonid Lubianitsky, a cameraman and television director, to make a short film of the tour. When giving Lubianitsky his instructions, he said, "There is a boy there, Misha Baryshnikov. Place special emphasis on him: he is

19

Misha's friend, Leonid Lubianitsky. New York. 1982.

a future genius." The young cameraman did not pay any particular attention at that time to the subject he was filming. Now Lubianitsky lives in the United States, having emigrated from the Soviet Union ten years ago, and works as a photographer. As a friend of Baryshnikov's he frequently photographs him onstage and off for American magazines.

Mikhail Baryshnikov danced his first solo when he was fifteen years old. Bella Kovarskaya, a teacher of character dance in the Riga Institute, was one of his ballet mistresses. Kovarskaya graduated from the Riga Choreographic Institute in 1955 with Yuris Kapralis, who with Natalia Leontyeva were Baryshnikov's first teachers of classical dance. Kovarskaya then joined Riga's ballet theater. In the year following her graduation, she began to teach at the school; for twenty-three years, she combined a performing career with work as a teacher. Kovarskaya emigrated to Canada in 1981, working as a guest teacher and rehearsal coach with professional Canadian and American companies. In 1982, she became the director of the Bayview School of Ballet in Toronto.

She described Misha Baryshnikov when he studied in her character dancing class in Riga during 1961 and 1962.

"Misha was an unusually gifted young boy. He always received a five [the highest mark in Soviet schools] in classical dance and a five in character dance. If it had been possible, I would have given him a five-plus. Kapralis provided Baryshnikov with the foundation of classical dance. Misha had such capable legs! In Kapralis's class he stood out both for his innate capabilities and for the purity of his execution of the technique. But as for Baryshnikov's noble manner of dancing onstage, I would like to think that this is the product of my work. Particularly in the character-dancing classes, I tried to inculcate a noble carriage and an assured stage presence in my pupils. In class, Misha responded so keenly to all corrections and took so much pleasure in what he was doing that it was a pleasure to teach him. Upon entering the classroom, I would always look to see where Misha was standing. His ever-smiling face became an inspiration to teach the lesson. Misha applied himself to the lessons of classical dance very diligently and very successfully; but it was specifically in character dancing that his expressiveness, his emotionality, and his soul emerged for the first time. I was convinced that he had a God-given talent for the dance. This impelled me to create a solo for him. In 1962, I staged *Tarantella* to Rossini's music. Misha danced the male solo with two little girls [one of them, Lora Lyubchenko, is now a leading ballerina with the Riga theater]. Misha danced this tarantella brilliantly and selflessly; the applause after his performance was thunderous. Everyone said, 'What a charming boy! How musical he is!' "

Misha began studying character dance with Valentin Blinov, also in Riga. That year Kovarskaya went to Leningrad, where she attended a two-year continuing-education program for ballet teachers at the Vaganova Institute. At the same time, she also taught classical and character dancing at the school. She often watched the classes of the remarkable Leningrad teacher of male dance, Aleksandr Pushkin, and took notes on his lessons (notes that, unfortunately, were confiscated at the border when she left the Soviet Union). But while in Leningrad, Kovarskaya did not forget her talented pupil, who she felt should study at the Vaganova school. In 1964, not long before the Latvian theater's tour to Leningrad, she approached Pushkin and said, "A young boy from the Riga ballet school, Misha Baryshnikov, is coming with the theater. Please take note of him!" Diana Joffe, a teacher at the Riga Institute who accompanied the children included in the Latvian theater's tour, actually

introduced Baryshnikov to Pushkin, and he was admitted to the Vaganova Institute.

In the fall of 1964, after Misha had entered the Leningrad school, Kovarskaya asked Pushkin how Baryshnikov was doing.

"Your protégé is an utterly astounding boy!" Pushkin replied.

In the Leningrad ballet school Baryshnikov was in Aleksandr Pushkin's classic-dance class, Igor Belsky's character-dance class, Valentina Osokina's acting class, and Nikolai Serebryanikov's lift class.

At the Vaganova Institute, the pupils present a concert twice a year. These concerts demonstrate the progress they have achieved during each semester. Misha was supposed to dance a variation from *Le Corsaire*. But Kovarskaya, who was still studying at the school, wanted to show her former student's versatility. She staged a solo for Baryshnikov, once again with two partners, in a Tyrolian dance. And again Misha had an enormous success in a character dance.

I first saw Mikhail Baryshnikov perform and took my first pictures of him quite accidentally in 1967, when he danced in his graduation performance from the Vaganova Choreographic Institute. Sasha Minz had gotten me a ticket in the first row of the orchestra so that I could photograph one of his friends.

The graduation performances always take place in June, on the stage of the Kirov Theater. The atmosphere in the theater is very solemn. The house is overfilled, packed with relatives and friends of the graduates. Teachers and ballet critics sit in the first rows of the orchestra and in the boxes in the first ring. In the boxes of all the higher tiers, balletomanes and students not appearing in the concert are seated shoulder to shoulder. The concert is long—about four hours—as each teacher strives to show his own pupils in a variety of aspects. It can be quite enjoyable when a new ballet is included in the program. But most of the concert consists of endless *pas de deux* and variations from the classical and contemporary repertory; moreover, these excerpts are the same from year to year. When a Rudolf Nureyev makes his debut in the *pas de deux* from

ABOVE LEFT. *Bella Kovarskaya and Yuris Kapralis dancing in their graduation performance in* Walpurgisnacht *from Gounod's opera* Faust. *Riga Choreographic Institute. 1955. They were Baryshnikov's first two teachers at the Riga ballet school.* ABOVE RIGHT. *Baryshnikov and Alexander Godunov among other pupils at the ballet school in Riga. From the left of the picture, Misha is the third kneeling boy; Godunov is in the same row, next to the girl with the braids.* ABOVE. *Mikhail Baryshnikov in his first solo on stage in* Tarantella. (*Photographs from the private collection of Bella Kovarskaya*)

ABOVE TOP AND BOTTOM. *Scenes from Aleksandr Pushkin's class staged for a television movie made in 1968, a year after Baryshnikov left the class. (From the private collection of Slava Santnaneev)*

RIGHT. *Baryshnikov loved the fencing classes in the Vaganova Institute ballet school in Leningrad. 1966.*

Le Corsaire, it is a gift to the audience. But entire graduations occur in which there is simply no one on whom to concentrate.

In the middle of the evening in June 1967, a student from the school, in the dress with a white pinafore that is the uniform of all female students in all Soviet schools, appeared onstage to announce the next number: the usual *pas de deux* from *Don Quixote.* I placed my camera in my lap and prepared to be bored. The first entrance of the young boy woke me up and made me reach for my camera.

This student stood out from the others immediately. Not only was the professionalism and purity of his technical execution rare for a graduating student, but his high and beautiful jumps were incredible. He did not run out onto the stage; he did not even fly out. He seemed to burst forth from the wings as if he had been shot from a catapult. He danced gaily and passionately, captivating us with his delight in pirouetting. He was not the interpreter of movement; he himself was movement, the dance. Exultant, he had the whole world before him.

"Who is this Baryshnikov?" I asked Sasha Minz after the performance. "What a good dancer he is!"

"Remember his name; you'll be hearing more about him," Minz replied.

There is a theater in America called the Met. The chandeliers, like sparkling hedgehog quills, hang low over the orchestra. As they rise to the ceiling, the curtain opens. Alexander Minz appears onstage in the black costume of Drosselmeyer. In this version of *The Nutcracker,* created by Mikhail Baryshnikov, Drosselmeyer is a storyteller and a magician, but he is not wicked. He loves, but does not rule over the love of others. The Nutcracker Prince in this production is only an invention of Drosselmeyer's and the Prince's spiritual world is hidden from us. When the battle with the mice ends, Drosselmeyer removes the distorted, smiling mask from the Nutcracker, and the pale, immobile, and suffering face of the Prince is revealed. The audience applauds both of them—Minz as Drosselmeyer and Baryshnikov as the Nutcracker. Thus I saw them, eventually, onstage together in America, in 1978.

Who could have imagined such a performance in 1967? The mass, legal emigration of the 1970s had not yet begun. And Soviet artists have never had the right to leave on their own initiative and work in another country. The very possibility of emigrating or defecting had not occurred to any of us at that time.

THE KIROV
THEATER

Is the weight of the century really at fault in this?
. . .Oh, Lord, is it possible
No one is guilty before anyone? . . .

—Yury Karabichevsky, epigraph
from *Metropol*, trans. by
H. William Tjalsma

T he Kirov, formerly the Mariinsky, was regarded as the finest ballet theater in Russia until the beginning of the sixties. It had an historic reputation: Marius Petipa and Mikhail Fokine had worked in this theater. The stars of Diaghilev's *Saisons Russes* had studied at the Petersburg ballet school. During the Soviet era, the Agrippina Vaganova Institute in Leningrad remained the best ballet school in the Soviet Union.

The Bolshoi Theater is known in the West because the Soviet government sends the capital's ballet company on tours abroad. (Perhaps the Ministry of Culture believes that since it is in the capital, it should be the best.) True, there were always fine stars and ballet masters at the Bolshoi Ballet; but the level of dancing, both of the principals and of the entire company, was always considered to be higher at the Leningrad theater. The Bolshoi often took not only stars from the Kirov (such as the great Galina Ulanova) but also ballet masters. The reason

29

for this was that the Kirov, in addition to preserving the now classic, but once innovative, ballets of Petipa in its repertory, also, as a rule, fostered new trends in choreography.

The ballet critic Poel Karp expressed a paradoxical thought when he wrote in his book *On Ballet,* "The Kirov Theater is the theater of established traditions, but the deepest of these is the tradition of innovation." Indeed, the history of Leningrad's ballet since the beginning of this century is the history of the struggle for change in choreography—and not only during the prerevolutionary period.

Until the beginning of the thirties, the daring Fedor Lopukhov—described by the great set and stage designer Alexander Benois as "gifted and fiery"—worked at the Kirov. In his experimentation, Lopukhov expanded the lexicon of classical dance with a new eurhythmic language, revived comic and grotesque ballet, and created the plotless, symphonic ballet form. When the Soviet authorities dismissed him from the directorship of the Kirov Theater for the first time in 1930, he did not lose heart. He received an invitation to head the nascent ballet company of the Maly Theater of Opera and Ballet, and proceeded to create a ballet theater with a repertory distinct from that of the Kirov. He worked tirelessly on his ideas, as if he sensed how little time was allotted to him for this work. In 1935, he staged his ballet *The Radiant Stream* to the music of Dmitry Shostakovich at the Bolshoi Theater in Moscow; it had already been performed at the Maly Theater to public acclaim. After the Moscow premiere, a *Pravda* editorial described Shostakovich's music as "formalistic," and Lopukhov's production as "balletic hypocrisy"—tantamount to a death sentence. Lopukhov's ballets were removed from the stage and these productions were virtually lost. But many of his choreographic compositions, which had provoked heated arguments at that time, were later used by other ballet masters; inconspicuously and anonymously, they became part of the heritage of Soviet choreography and even of the programs of the ballet school. Lopukhov's ideas sustain choreographers to this day.

New ballet masters emerged to take the place of the banned Lopukhov, and a new direction in ballet developed, the so-called *drambalet* or drama ballet, in which dancing served to illustrate a subject. Dance was allotted a role secondary to the story. The dancing was often an accom-

ABOVE LEFT. *Galina Ulanova and Konstantin Sergeyev in* Giselle. *Kirov Theater. 1940s.*
ABOVE RIGHT. *Yury Grigorovich. 1972.*

The Legend of Love. *Choreographer: Grigorovich. Kirov Theater. 1962.*

paniment to a dramatic production without words. The innovators of this new trend, Rostislav Zakharov (ballet master at the Bolshoi from 1936 to 1956) and Leonid Lavrovsky (the artistic director of the Bolshoi Ballet from 1944 to 1964), who had both graduated from the Leningrad Institute during the twenties, also started their careers at the Kirov Theater. Before their removal to the Bolshoi, both choreographers created their best ballets at the Kirov; these works, Zakharov's *The Fountain of Bakhchisarai* (1934) and Lavrovsky's *Romeo and Juliet* (1940), became "classics" of drama ballet. Afterward, the two transferred these ballets to the Bolshoi.

What was detrimental to the dance in the Soviet Union was not so much that the contemporary language of choreography stopped developing but that drama ballet was proclaimed to be the *only* acceptable direction in Soviet ballet. Diversity of balletic forms was essentially forbidden. However, during its early years, the evolution of drama ballet was not entirely predictable.

Throughout the Stalinist era, all of the arts were limited to the expression of meaning in realistic form; art was intended to show life to the Soviet people in a cheerful, optimistic light. Paradoxically, since the nature of the art of ballet in itself is very far from the principles of Socialist Realism, even the most official trend, drama ballet bore at first a slightly nonconformist character. Zakharov and Lavrovsky, who were completely loyal to the regime, chose from the classics of world and Russian literature stories with tragic endings, rather than optimistic ones, for their ballets.

Undoubtedly, the most outstanding ballerina in this genre was Galina Ulanova. In the same period there were many extremely talented dancers, but she alone was a genius. Ulanova expressed the moral ideal of her time, although she herself did not recognize it. Her heroines died at the will of the choreographers, but not only did the Maria, Corala, or Juliet created by Ulanova die; in each ballet, our peer died before our eyes, neither resisting evil nor submitting to it. At that time, when it seemed that terror had destroyed all normal, human feelings and instincts, Ulanova's art conveyed an elevated moral strength that would survive death and destruction by the state.

By the beginning of the fifties, drama ballet had turned into a parody

Igor Belsky. 1973.

of itself, the performances degenerating into pantomime with dances. It had also become the obstacle to any fresh choreographic ideas. Nevertheless, at this time a distinguished ballet master, Leonid Yakobson, whom Baryshnikov considers to be the most talented of all Soviet choreographers, began working at the Kirov Theater.

In 1957, a genuine revolution in ballet finally occurred at the Kirov, with the staging of Yury Grigorovich and Igor Belsky's first ballets. These two events signified the end of the era of drama ballet in Leningrad and marked the return of symphonic dancing to the stage. The fledgling ballet masters openly acknowledged Fedor Lopukhov as the teacher through whom they had inherited the legacy of Fokine and Petipa. In the ensuing atmosphere of creativity, young dancers and established stars alike flourished. But by 1967, when Baryshnikov came to the stage, the theater was once again in a state of decay. What had happened during those ten years?

In the Soviet Union, ignorant and unsophisticated people, fearing the new and the unfamiliar, stand in the way of any progress in art.

Osipenko as Cleopatra in Antony and Cleopatra. *1968.*

Konstantin Sergeyev (a principal dancer from 1931 to 1961) and his wife, Natalia Dudinskaya (a principal from 1931 to 1962), were, in effect, the stooges of the party leaders in the Kirov Theater. Sergeyev had been an official ballet master in the theater since 1946, the head ballet master from 1951 to 1955, and the artistic director from 1960 to 1970. Enjoying the confidence of Soviet authorities, he was the sole master of ballet. A mediocre choreographer and a staunch apologist of drama ballet, Sergeyev did his best to prevent the works of other ballet masters from being staged at the theater. Grigorovich's debut took place only because he had the support of Lopukhov, who served once again as the artistic director of ballet at the Kirov from 1951 to 1956. Lopukhov, a person of enormous talent and great generosity, whether at work or in disgrace, always encouraged the projects of other choreographers and tried to help them in their work. Sergeyev, on the contrary, did not permit such talented ballet masters as Igor Chernyshev and Georgi Aleksidze (whose best ballets were short works) to stage their creations at the Kirov. Sergeyev could not oppose the work of Grigorovich and Belsky, since the success of their first ballets had been tremendous and because drama ballet itself had become too compromised. But Sergeyev applied massive pressure at the

FACING PAGE. *Osipenko as the Mistress of Copper Mountain in* The Stone Flower. *c. 1969.*

37

Ministry of Culture, where he was favored over the recalcitrant Lopukhov, in order to remove new ballet masters from the theater.

Lopukhov was again dismissed from the directorship in 1956, this time on the pretext of retirement. In 1964, Yury Grigorovich, who had by this time staged his second ballet, *The Legend of Love,* was sent into honorary exile to direct the Bolshoi Ballet. Grigorovich was never permitted to work at the Kirov Theater again. It was by this act that Baryshnikov's fate was sealed.

Grigorovich was a product of the Leningrad school and a former dancer of the Leningrad ballet; he had already found ardent and likeminded collaborators among the artists, and the Leningrad audiences loved him (many people continued to go to Moscow just to see his new productions). Grigorovich truly revived the Bolshoi Ballet; he staged wonderful productions of *The Nutcracker* and *Spartacus,* although his subsequent ballets were not so successful. If he had not had to direct the enormous and complicated collective of the Bolshoi Theater, nor submit to the Ministry of Culture because of this responsibility—in short, if he had been working with the conditions of creative freedom that Western choreographers have—he might have become the Russian Béjart.

Belsky was appointed the artistic director of the Maly Theater. Having ended up in a secondary company, he neither lost heart nor stopped taking his creativity seriously. He gave young ballet masters access to his theater, in contrast to the policies of the Kirov. But during his eleven years of work in the Maly, Belsky himself created only two or three truly interesting ballets.

Briefly, by the middle of the sixties, the Kirov Ballet was in a muddled state. Sergeyev's ballets lacked originality, and he began to borrow eclectically from more creative choreographers. From time to time Sergeyev invited other ballet masters (usually old masters of drama ballet) to stage works. And Leonid Yakobson staged new ballets only once every two or three years.

In order to satisfy the demand for new repertory, Sergeyev occupied himself throughout his tenure with the alteration of the classical ballets. The Kirov Theater truly does preserve the best ballets of the past in its repertory and also the noble manner of performing these works—although, according to ballet historians, only *Giselle* is still performed in

Nikita Dolgushin in rehearsal at the Philharmonic Hall in Leningrad. 1969.

a version similar to that of Petipa. Yet after the revolution, Lopukhov had tried assiduously to restore the masterpieces of the classic legacy. In cooperation with the composer Boris Asafiev and the designer Alexander Benois, he revived *The Sleeping Beauty*. He composed lost dances and variations, using the recollections of former participants, with such respect and understanding of Petipa's work that they fit organically into these ballets. Sergeyev, in contrast, reworked the ballets of other artists without any apparent or creative benefit. He spoiled *The Sleeping Beauty* when he redid the act featuring the Nereids. He ruined Petipa's *corps de ballet* ensembles and deprived the dancing of its romantic animation in adapting it to the capabilities of his partner, Dudinskaya. She was a ballerina of virtuosity suited to heroic roles, but with no aptitude for lyrical-romantic parts.

A stultifying atmosphere existed in the theater at the beginning of

39

the sixties. Only because of a struggle by the other ballerinas against Dudinskaya's monopoly of all the major roles in new ballets did the aging prima finally retire from the stage. Then the younger dancers gained access to all of the leading parts. But Sergeyev remained in control. Still, almost no new, interesting works entered the repertory. As a result, beginning in 1961, the half dozen finest dancers left the theater: Rudolf Nureyev and Nikita Dolgushin in 1961, Natalia Makarova in 1970, Alla Osipenko in 1971, and Mikhail Baryshnikov in 1974. Yury Soloviev shot himself in 1977.

It is not an exaggeration to say that Dolgushin and Osipenko, although unknown to Western audiences, were dancers of the highest rank.

Alla Osipenko left the Kirov at the height of her career. She had an amazingly beautiful body and a proud grace in her movements, and would have been a star in any of the best companies in the world. Soon after her graduation in 1950, Osipenko began dancing solo parts. Her performances in the secondary role of the Lilac Fairy in *The Sleeping Beauty* accustomed audiences to expect no less than another star in the role of Aurora. Nevertheless, the true depth of this actress emerged in the ballets of Grigorovich. She was unquestionably the best Mistress of the Copper Mountain (*The Stone Flower*, 1957) in both Leningrad and Moscow and a tremendous Mekhmene Banu (*The Legend of Love*). There were few artists who interpreted Grigorovich's choreography as eloquently as Osipenko did. The public reason for her departure from the theater was the disrespect and rudeness with which Petr Rachinsky, the administrative director, treated her. But Osipenko resolved on this brave step because she felt the emptiness of her creative life. She was tired of dancing, year after year, the same classical ballets and the works created for her at the beginning of her career.

She danced in Igor Chernyshev's ballet *Antony and Cleopatra* (music by E. Lazarev) at the Maly Theater in 1968 and left the Kirov in 1971. At first she worked with the Choreographic Miniatures Ensemble directed by Yakobson, a company whose repertory consists of short works; later, she joined a newly created ballet collective under the leadership of the young ballet master Boris Eifman (this group is now very popular in the Soviet Union). For a long time after leaving the Kirov, she was

FACING PAGE. *Natalia Makarova as Odette and Nikita Dolgushin as Siegfried in* Swan Lake. *Kirov Theater. 1968.*

41

Makarova as Juliet, Anatoly Nisnevich as Romeo. Romeo and Juliet. *1964.*

RIGHT. *Makarova as Princess Florine in* The Sleeping Beauty. *1965.* FACING PAGE. *Makarova as Raymonda, Svyatoslav Kuznetsov as the Eastern prince Abdurakhman in* Raymonda. *Music by Glazunov, choreography by Petipa; revived by Konstantin Sergeyev. 1970.*

Makarova in Syrinx, *a short work to the music of Benjamin Britten, staged for her by Georgi Aleksidze. 1968.*

afraid to enter its auditorium, even as a spectator, to see the stage where she no longer worked. All the same, she returned to dance with Baryshnikov in his last premiere there.

Nikita Dolgushin was not simply a talented dancer; he also possessed a unique artistic personality. His dancing was truly lyrical, distinguished by an innate refinement and intellectuality, like that of no other dancer in the Soviet Union. During his second year at the Kirov, he danced Albrecht in *Giselle,* and someone in the theater remarked that he resembled Sergeyev as a young man. This totally inaccurate observation sealed Dolgushin's fate, for Sergeyev could not forgive the young dancer for this comparison. No more new roles were given to Dolgushin and he was not included in a trip abroad with the company. Dolgushin, feeling the dancer's time pressure, made a daring decision: he left the Kirov in 1961 and went not to the West but to the East, to join the theater of opera and ballet in the distant Siberian city of Novosibirsk. When he returned to Leningrad in 1968, he was already famous throughout the ballet world in the Soviet Union as a superlative classical dancer and, possibly, the best interpreter at that time of the modern repertory (in particular, the ballets of Grigorovich and the young Oleg Vinogradov).

It seemed that the doors of any theater should have been open to him. But Sergeyev offered Dolgushin only a trial of three performances, *Giselle* and *Swan Lake* with Natalia Makarova and *The Legend of Love* with Emma Minchenok and Alla Osipenko. The people who saw these performances must remember them to this day. His *pas de deux* with Makarova confirmed the impression that they had made together at their graduation performance: these two artists were born to dance with each other. Dolgushin received tremendous acclaim, but he was not taken into the theater. Sergeyev declared, according to the other dancers, that Dolgushin had acquired provincial manners in Novosibirsk. Deeply disappointed, Dolgushin joined the Maly Opera Theater, where he continued to work at full strength. In fact, Dolgushin's repertory, both classical and contemporary, at the Maly Theater in those years was much more varied than that of his peers at the Kirov. And Dolgushin's roles in the new ballets of Oleg Vinogradov, as Prince Igor in *Yaroslavna* or the Prince in *Cinderella,* are among the most significant in Soviet ballet history. But on the stage of a secondary theater, without an adequate partner or a sufficiently professional company in the background, Dolgushin looked like a guest artist at all of his performances. The dancer's pride must

45

have suffered badly. As a rule, those who were not chosen by the Kirov went to work at the Maly. And there, at the illustrious Kirov, the young boy Misha Baryshnikov was easily and freely developing into what Dolgushin should have become: the leading dancer of the theater.

Dolgushin made compromises. He even agreed to dance the role of Hamlet in Sergeyev's eclectic and uninteresting ballet of the same name, when no other artists would do so. He did this simply to have the opportunity to dance on the stage of the Kirov. Dolgushin's name on the poster drew the public. But still Sergeyev did not offer him a place in the theater. When Sergeyev was removed from the artistic directorship of the Kirov, Vinogradov, as Leningrad's next leading ballet master, was forced to leave the Maly Opera, where he had much more creative freedom. But Vinogradov did not take Dolgushin with him to the Kirov. Today, Dolgushin is over forty years old; even if he is still dancing, his career is practically over.

Natalia Makarova graduated from the ballet institute with Dolgushin in 1959; both of them had already attracted attention in a performance prior to their graduation of *Lisztiana,* a one-act ballet staged for them by Kasian Goleisovsky. Makarova did not open up onstage at first. She was a "difficult child" in the ballet family of the Kirov Theater: lacking purity of technique, she strove to dance everything in her own way. Fedor Lopukhov and the ballet critic Vera Krasovskaya noticed her immediately, but the active ballet masters did not include her in their works. Only Yakobson gave the young dancer roles early on in her career. First she danced Zoya in *The Bedbug* and afterward the Beautiful Maiden in *Country of Wonder.* The part of Zoya was small and "nonclassical," but Makarova shone in it, perhaps more impressively than in her classical roles at that time. Her particular ability to project the music in every cell of her body helped her when she danced Juliet in the drama ballet *Romeo and Juliet* by Leonid Lavrovsky. Makarova did not copy Ulanova, as almost all the young ballerinas did. And although Lavrovsky's choreography was totally unsuited to her, Makarova danced in harmony with Prokofiev's tragic music. Makarova's Juliet was an unfortunate girl, protesting against the constraints of her era. She was talented; she was alone. She was Natasha Makarova caught in the intrigues of the ballet world surrounding her. In general, the theme of Makarova's roles at the time was often

a combination of defenselessness and audacious revolt. In the classical repertory she was irresistible as Princess Florine in *The Sleeping Beauty.* But her entire Leningrad career was, as was Nureyev's, a prelude to her real blossoming in the West.

Misha Baryshnikov had the opportunity to dance with Makarova in only one short work. But he often danced with Alla Sizova, who had graduated from the Vaganova Institute in 1958, one year earlier than Makarova. What a brilliant career was predicted for her at her graduation performance! That evening she danced with Rudolf Nureyev and shared his success in the *pas de deux* from *Le Corsaire.* Sizova was beautifully trained and richly talented; she had a high, broad jump with phenomenal *ballon* and *élévation,* and beautiful lines in her *arabesques.* Her dancing was tender, soft, and graceful. During the early sixties she often came to my home with Sasha Minz, who was in love with her.

At the age of twenty-one she injured her back from overwork while on tour in New York. She did not dance for about two years. When she returned to the stage, it was clear that the rapid progress of Sizova's career had come abruptly to a halt with her injury. The partner of two outstanding Russian dancers, Nureyev and Baryshnikov, and a prima ballerina of the Kirov Theater, she continued to dance almost all of the classical and contemporary repertory. But in none of these ballets did she fulfill her early promise. With the passage of time, her youthful charm and virginal tenderness could no longer substitute for artistic maturity. Quietly, modestly, and without any dramatic failures, she is dancing out her ballet life.

47

THE FIRST
KIROV YEARS

*Whether someone will soon emerge who, by rights, will deserve . . .
the sobriquet "God of the dance," I do not know. In the meanwhile,
I see that one such dancer is developing. And his fate is
entirely in the hands of the theater.*

—Fedor Lopukhov, "Notes
of a Ballet Master"

Baryshnikov graduated from the Vaganova Choreographic Institute in 1967 and joined the ballet company of the Kirov Theater. I do not remember who introduced me to Misha. My first personal recollection of Misha is of running into him shortly after his graduation performance, not far from his home. We greeted each other as acquaintances. He was walking with a friend—a short girl with a voice so low she sounded almost like a man—who was holding an aromatic package of freshly ground coffee. We stopped to chat and we discovered that Misha and I were neighbors. The Kirov had given him a room in a communal apartment on the Petrograd Side, one block from mine (in addition to Misha, a family lived in the apartment). Gradually Misha became a frequent guest in our home. He would drop in to see us at any time, even when returning home late at night, if he saw the lights in our windows. My husband and I would cook *pelmeni* (dumplings) for him. At that time he was happy and loved to make jokes. He

49

ABOVE. *The apartment building on Kolpinskaya Street (on the Petrograd Side) where Baryshnikov lived after graduating from the Vaganova Institute. His apartment was on the first floor; the windows looked right out onto the street.*
ABOVE RIGHT. *The apartment house on the corner of the Moika Canal and Dzerzhinsky Street to which Misha moved in 1972. The entrance to the staircase that led to his apartment was located in the courtyard.*

Misha with Foma as a puppy. 1972.

was inquisitive and managed to attend all of the most interesting new ballets and dramatic performances, to see new films, and to read new books. There was a thirst for life and a merry readiness for adventure in him.

The room in which Misha lived was rather bare. He was poor and had almost no furniture. The apartment was located on the first floor and the window looked out onto a street with an ever-present pile of garbage on the opposite curb.

There on the Petrograd Side, I met Slava Santnaneev and other of Misha's friends, including Tatyana (Tanya) Koltsova, who graduated from the Vaganova Institute one year after Misha. Tanya confided to me that Misha began to court her while she was still a student in the school. In the beginning she avoided Misha, embarrassed by the fact that he was already an emerging star and that she was no one. She felt wary of a serious relationship. Nevertheless, when Misha received a new apartment from the theater in the beginning of 1972, she moved in as his wife. This is not unusual in Russia. When young people live together and take their relationship seriously, their friends consider them husband and wife.

Misha's new studio apartment was located in a beautiful area in Leningrad, on the corner of the Moika Canal and Dzerzhinsky Street, within walking distance of the theater. Misha soon acquired a white standard poodle puppy named Foma, who had been born in February 1972; Slava brought him to Misha in March. Later, a black cat named Anfisa took up residence in Misha and Tanya's home. When Misha and Tanya separated, Tanya took Anfisa with her.

One of Baryshnikov's first roles at the Kirov Theater was that of the Youth, the Friend of Asiat, in *Goryanka,* a new ballet by Oleg Vinogradov. Baryshnikov made his debut in *Don Quixote* in 1969, dancing this ballet with Ninel Kurgapkina, who was nineteen years older than he. Kurgapkina was technically a strong ballerina and, after Dudinskaya, was the leading Kitri of the Kirov Ballet. If she has not yet retired from the stage, she no doubt is still dancing this role. During the seventies, Misha danced *Don Quixote* with Svetlana Yefremova, a short, young dancer of the "ingenue" type. I did not care for her in ballerina parts, especially alongside of Baryshnikov. But when I made this remark to Misha he

responded irritably, "And with whom should I dance? Well, tell me, name one. With whom?" And he was right. There was not one young virtuoso ballerina for the role of Kitri in the theater at that time.

Misha danced that first performance of *Don Quixote* and all of the following ones daringly and superbly in terms of technique; the more he danced, the greater his perfection. The public loved him in this ballet. He was undoubtedly and indisputably the best Basil in Leningrad, right up to his defection. But only in America did I see Baryshnikov dance Basil in all the splendor of his technical perfection. When he danced the variation that he had staged for the tavern scene, it seemed as if his feet did not touch the floor once the entire time. I remember one performance when the entire audience in the Metropolitan Opera House gasped in unison, "Ah-ah? ah-ah Ah!"

During the early years of his career, Misha danced Yakobson's short work *Vestris* in concert performances with invariable success. Yakobson had staged this work especially for Baryshnikov for the 1969 International Ballet Competition in Moscow. Yakobson, a great discoverer of talent, revealed Baryshnikov's capacity for dramatic acting and transformations. In *Vestris* Baryshnikov first displayed both a fine artistic intuition and an innate flair for performing modern, grotesque movements.

In 1969 Baryshnikov appeared as Mercutio in a one-act production of *Romeo and Juliet,* set to the music of Berlioz. Igor Chernyshev, a principal dancer at the Kirov, choreographed this ballet. It was performed during Irina Kolpakova's "creative evening."

Irina Kolpakova, prima ballerina of the Kirov Theater, graduated from the Choreographic Institute in 1951 (with the last class of the famous Russian teacher Agrippina Vaganova) and is still dancing today. She gradually moved up from solo variations to the interpretation of the major parts in the classical ballets. Kolpakova's love for hard work, in combination with an innate gift and a magnificent command of technique, made her the leading ballerina of the Kirov. Onstage she was charming and graceful and the critics called her dancing crystal-clear. Moreover, Kolpakova could interpret almost any style of choreography. But, as an actress, Kolpakova was phlegmatic and her lyricism bordered on the childish. Of course, her work with Grigorovich in his ballets *The Stone Flower* (as Katerina) and *The Legend of Love* (as Shirin) brought her not only great fame but also stirred her creative imagination. Still, for many viewers, her artistic naïveté and lack of emotion detracted from her merits not only in contemporary but also in classical ballets.

Feeling the shortcomings in the contemporary repertory, as did Baryshnikov and many other artists, Kolpakova never passed up an opportunity to work with new choreographers, regardless of whether the performance would take place in the theater or in a concert hall.

A "creative evening" was a safety valve for the artists. Whenever the theater came to an impasse, the leading soloists who were suffering from a lack of work would secure permission to produce an evening of ballet for themselves. Irina Kolpakova was apparently the first to do this, in 1969. On this occasion, she invited the young ballet masters Oleg Vinogradov and Gogi Aleksidze and the dancer Igor Chernyshev to work with her. Chernyshev had already staged *Romeo and Juliet* with Natalia Makarova and Vadim Gulyaev in the leading roles and with Mikhail Baryshnikov as Mercutio. The work was not part of the theater's scheduled season. In other words, the dancers rehearsed without pay and in addition to their regular workloads. Sergeyev, after seeing a rehearsal of *Romeo and Juliet*, would not permit it to be performed on the stage of the theater, saying that the Soviet public did not need to see decadence. (Makarova describes this incident in detail in her book, *A Dance Autobiography*.) Since Kolpakova was a member of the Communist Party, she

53

ABOVE LEFT, RIGHT, AND
FACING PAGE. *Basil in* Don
Quixote. *1969–1970.*

occupied a privileged position among the dancers. Therefore, she obtained permission to present *Romeo and Juliet* in her creative evening and thus danced Juliet at the Kirov in place of Makarova. (Of course, Igor Chernyshev would have preferred Makarova to dance Juliet instead of Kolpakova, but what could he do? He was forced to compromise or risk never seeing his ballet on the stage.)

Baryshnikov danced Mercutio. Misha, at that period in his life, displayed many of Mercutio's characteristics: youthful energy, a radiant light, and joy. Even before Misha's appearance in the role of Mercutio, the young Moscow critic Alexander Demidov wrote in *Evening Leningrad,* "His dancing is an absorbing, intensive pursuit of the elusive beauty of art, the endless aspiration toward an ideal." This statement precisely defines Baryshnikov's creative work at that time.

In 1970, Konstantin Sergeyev staged *Hamlet* to the music of Nikolai Chervinsky. After having danced two or three performances, Baryshnikov refused to appear further in the work. Misha declared at a meeting of the ballet company that he could not stand for half an hour in an

55

As Basil, with Ninel Kurgapkina as Kitri, in Don Quixote.

Misha Baryshnikov performing with Svetlana Efremova the pas de deux *from* Le Corsaire, *in 1969, during his first year in the theater.*

ABOVE LEFT. *As Hamlet.*
ABOVE. *As Vestris in*
Yakobson's Vestris.

attitude that signified, "To be or not to be." Other artists told me that Sergeyev was perplexed. He sincerely did not understand why anyone would refuse to dance the leading role in his ballet. I think that Misha already sensed the strength of his position: since Nureyev had defected to the West, there was not another dancer at the Kirov who was equal to Baryshnikov. However, it was not just a matter of his self-awareness as an artist. Psychologically, Misha was always a free person. Subsequently, he challenged those in authority at the Kirov several times. But this refusal was the first act of defiance, the first manifestation of the free soul of the young dancer.

Other than *Don Quixote*, not one of the ballets from this early period was retained in Baryshnikov's repertory. In March 1971, the premiere of *The Creation of the World*, in which Misha danced the role of Adam, took place. With this premiere, the next period of Baryshnikov's creative development began. Or perhaps it would be more accurate to say that, with this premiere, the Baryshnikov who is known to the West was born.

57

THE CREATION OF THE WORLD

The Creation of the World, *a ballet in three acts, inspired by the satirical drawings of J. Effel. Music by A. Petrov; conceived and choreographed by V. Vasiliev and N. Kasatkina; March 23, 1971; Kirov Theater; scenes and costumes by E. Stenburg; conducted by V. Fedotov. Adam, V. Gulyaev; Eve, N. Bolshakova; God, Yu. Soloviev.*

—Ballet Encyclopedia

T he facts provided in the Soviet *Ballet Encyclopedia* about the history of Effel's ballet *The Creation of the World* do not coincide entirely with those from a more accurate document, the program actually distributed at the premiere of the ballet on March 23, 1971, in Leningrad. In the program, the following cast was listed: Adam, Mikhail Baryshnikov, not Vadim Gulyaev; Eve, Irina Kolpakova, not Natalia Bolshakova; the Devil (not even mentioned in the encyclopedia), Valery Panov; God, Yury Soloviev, as stated. But, according to the encyclopedia, Baryshnikov and Panov never existed. Nor, to judge by other entries, do Makarova and Nureyev. They were never in Leningrad and they are not now in any other ballet company in the world. How comical it is—and yet how distasteful it must have been to the contributors to sign their names to such "facts."

Despite the disinformation given in the *Ballet Encyclopedia*, *The Crea-*

59

tion of the World played an important role in Misha's artistic development in Leningrad.

The 1970–1971 season was a happy one for the entire company. The work on a new, contemporary ballet had finally brought the troupe a long-awaited success. (Three years had gone by since the creation of a major work, *Goryanka* by Oleg Vinogradov, considered worth retaining in the repertory. That ballet continues to be performed at the Kirov to the present day.)

Natalia Kasatkina and her husband, Vladimir Vasiliev, dancers with the Bolshoi Ballet, conceived the idea for *The Creation of the World* from Jean Effel's satirical drawings on biblical themes. The ballet was a lively choreographic narration of the story from *Genesis*. God creates the earth while the Devil, out of boredom, tries to impede him. After that, Adam is created and then Eve, from Adam's rib. Adam and Eve, contrary to the biblical version, discover love not by tasting the forbidden fruit but while trying to grasp it from the Devil, who was teasing them. This love impels them to abandon the Garden of Eden to see the world with their own eyes. Then the Devil and the She-Devil stir up a tempest that they are unable to stop and, ultimately, die in the worldwide cataclysm. Adam and Eve survive and realize their love for one another.

Not long ago, Misha said to me that his recollection was that the

beginning of *The Creation of the World* was blasphemous, but the middle section was very "cute." In my opinion, there was no blasphemy, either in Effel's sly and ironical—but endearing—drawings or in the ballet itself. Rather, the production was simply very uneven. The first act, until Adam's appearance, was drawn out and dull, except for the scenes with God, which were quite entertaining. The best part of the ballet was the middle—depicting the blissful life of Adam and Eve in the Garden of Eden—a section filled with unexpected, witty staging and choreographic devices. And although the *pas de deux* of Adam and Eve on earth, after leaving the Garden, made a pleasant impression, it was followed by an utterly feeble ending. The composer had, for some reason, incorporated the music of "The Ode to Joy" from Beethoven's Ninth Symphony into the last scene—a horrendous misjudgment.

But, despite its unevenness, *The Creation of the World* was very popular with the public. It was a cheerful production without any pretense to serious philosophy. While not successful in all aspects, it was still a skillful effort in which the dancers received the opportunity to work in a free, contemporary style. (Throughout the ballet, Eve danced on *demi-pointe* without shoes, in the style of a modern dancer.) *The Creation of the World* was remarkable for its superior performances, not only among the principals, but also among the young dancers appearing in the ensemble. Both the public and the critics immediately singled out one of the angels, the young Lyudmilla Semenyaka. She graduated from the Vaganova Choreographic Institute in 1970 and is now a superstar with the Bolshoi Ballet.

The young principals, Vadim Gulyaev and Natalia Bolshakova, who are listed in the *Ballet Encyclopedia* as the creators of the roles of Adam and Eve, actually did dance them, but in the second cast. Gulyaev, who graduated from the Vaganova Institute one year before Baryshnikov, was—and still is—a talented artist, although more suited to modern rather than classical choreography. Kasatkina and Vasiliev did begin staging the first scene with Gulyaev as Adam. Misha was ill at the time and did not begin to rehearse until later.

Other dancers working on *The Creation of the World* recounted that when Baryshnikov first came to rehearsal and saw how easily Gulyaev turned his "soft" legs out into *écarté,* he cried out, "What are you doing?!

FACING PAGE, TOP AND BOTTOM. *God creates Adam. God: Soloviev.*

RIGHT, BELOW, AND FACING PAGE, TOP LEFT AND BOTTOM. *The first movements of Adam as a child. Archangel: Evgeny Shcherbakov; Angels: Nina Sakhnovskaya, Lyudmilla Semenyaka; God: Soloviev.*

FACING PAGE, TOP RIGHT. *Adam is crying; he wants to sleep. God calls the "nanny angels." From left to right, God: Soloviev; Archangel: Vladimir Ponomarev; Adam: Baryshnikov.*

I can't do that!" In general the rehearsals with the two casts developed into an unacknowledged competition between the two pairs of performers of Adam and Eve. For all four artists, their appearance in this ballet became landmarks in their careers.

Panov, captivated by his role from the start, was especially memorable during the rehearsals, and quite funny in the seriousness with which he parodied the cliché of devils in ballet stories. Later, onstage, he created a perfect caricature. Although other interpreters of the Devil executed accurately and conscientiously everything that the choreography demanded, they did not have Panov's simple mastery or his sense of humor. Proving himself a worthy counterpart to the other artists, Panov brought the role to life. With his departure from the production, the scenes with the Devil suffered noticeably.

Usually, before a premiere at the Kirov Theater, there are two dress rehearsals onstage, attended by invited audiences. The first run-through is a rough rehearsal during which the lighting is improved, the conductor adjusts the tempi, and the dancers get accustomed to their costumes. The tickets to the first run-through are not numbered and are given out, free, to all present and former theater employees and artists. Spectators sit wherever they can find a seat. The first ten to fifteen rows of the orchestra and the forward boxes of the first and second tiers are cordoned off, reserved for company dancers who are not in the production and for theater administrators. Taking photographs is permitted at this rehearsal. Occasionally, a second run-through—"for papas and mamas"—is held; the tickets for this rehearsal are distributed to the artists appearing in the production. A "general rehearsal," or preview, is last.

Stage rehearsals with audiences start at 11:30 A.M. or at 12:00 noon. The preview is conducted solemnly; it is almost the premiere. Employees of the Ministry of Culture and of other Soviet institutions sit in the first row. They either "accept" or "do not accept" the work—they permit it to be premiered, or demand a reworking of the production to improve the ideological content. Critics and other officials are also invited. The first cast dances in this performance. As a rule, the first run-through is given to the second cast. Therefore, Gulyaev and Bolshakova danced at the first rehearsal on March 19, 1971, and Baryshnikov and Kolpakova at the preview on March 20.

FACING PAGE. *Adam is bored.*

66

The Devil brings Adam a girl friend, the She-Devil, for games. The She-Devil: Svetlana Yefremova; the Devil: Valery Panov.

Bolshakova looked very pretty on stage as Eve. A long-legged, shapely woman with enormous eyes and long, blond hair, she was both funny and charming in her role. Her Eve was a woman who quickly mastered the science of ruling her Adam. Gulyaev danced his part beautifully, communicating all of the nuances of Adam's feelings sensitively and expressively.

Having seen Bolshakova and Gulyaev in *The Creation of the World,* everyone awaited with even greater interest the preview with Baryshnikov and Kolpakova.

On March 20, I arrived at the theater with my seven-year-old son, Igor. When I approached the door with the tickets in my hand, the usher would not take them, saying, "Children are not allowed."

"Why not?" I asked in surprise. "It is a morning rehearsal." (No one under the age of sixteen is allowed to attend evening theater performances in the Soviet Union.)

The usher looked at me reproachfully and glanced at my son. Then she said to me meaningfully, "Have you yourself seen the ballet? It is absolutely impossible to let a child see it." The usher must have considered the modern, tight-fitting leotards and, in particular, the placement of the flowers on the costumes of Adam and Eve immoral. She must have also been shocked by the scene in which they first meet. Adam and Eve express their surprise naïvely and openly as they discover the similarities and differences between their bodies.

FACING PAGE. Adam in ecstasy over his new friends.

68

I insisted, and we were admitted, since the guardian of morality could

TOP, MIDDLE, AND RIGHT.
*Adam's jump, devised by
Baryshnikov.*

LEFT. *God created another girl friend for Adam, Eve, in order to divert Adam from bad company. Eve: Irina Kolpakova.* BELOW. *Adam caught sight of Eve. "Who is this?!"*

Eve: Kolpakova; Adam: Baryshnikov.

The Devil appeals very much to Eve. Eve: Kolpakova; Adam: Baryshnikov; the Devil: Valery Panov.

not officially prohibit me from attending a morning rehearsal with a child.

We sat down in our box. The curtain went up, and the first act began. Soon thereafter, Baryshnikov was slowly somersaulting, trying to coordinate his arms and legs, and looking out into the house with the blank gaze of a small child.

The audience laughed as Adam seriously inspected his feet and, like an infant, tried to stuff one of them into his mouth. Baryshnikov's performance of Adam as a child, with his caprices and mischief, his meeting with Eve, and the game of tag, had such ease and authentic emotional intensity that he conjured up the illusion of a child's bewilderment. His Adam was simultaneously funny and touching. The game with the She-Devil, the first woman Adam ever sees, sets off an explosion of emotions in him that he does not yet understand. The happiness of the small child is soon transformed into the exultation of a teenager who has just discovered an extravagant new game, all the more exciting for being forbidden. To express this youthful joy, Baryshnikov devised an astounding cascade of jumps like aerial somersaults, created from a *grand jeté en tournant*, but executed with a revolution in the air backward over his head. No one could repeat these miraculous leaps.

The Devil and the She-Devil tease Adam and Eve with the fruit of wisdom, an apple. In pursuit of this apple, Adam and Eve discover love. Demanding the apple, Adam holds out his hand to the Devil, a childish look of insistence on his face. Then, no longer a child, he turns to Eve. Kolpakova as Eve did not have Baryshnikov's range of feelings, but she seemed to come to an involuntary standstill upon seeing Adam transformed and his face animated with emotions.

Baryshnikov's interpretation of Adam secured his place as the first of the leading artists of the Kirov Ballet. There was no longer any doubt that Baryshnikov was a unique phenomenon, a dancer of the highest caliber. Before *The Creation of the World*, it was evident that Misha had enormous potential; but in this ballet Misha showed, lightly and playfully, the true extent of his capabilities. Earlier, in roles such as Basil in *Don Quixote* or Mercutio in *Romeo and Juliet*, indications of his abilities had been manifested. His brilliant virtuosity, *ballon*, *élévation*, and consummate placement in every pose at any moment of the dance were all evident. He delighted in his own dancing and had a natural ability to

73

God, the happy Father (Soloviev), and an Angel (Lyudmilla Semenyaka). Semenyaka graduated from the Vaganova Institute in 1970. She is now a superstar at the Bolshoi Ballet in Moscow.

While God and the Angels rejoice at the creation of the first people, the Devil tempts Adam and Eve with an apple. From left to right, Adam: Baryshnikov; Eve: Kolpakova; the Devil: Vadim Budarin; the She-Devil: Tatyana Legat.

74

create the illusion of total effortlessness. Further, in his leaps, he seemed to defy gravity and hover over the earth. All of these qualities now merged into an artistic whole, while the splendid extravagance of youth began to mature into a discriminating acting method.

Usually, Kolpakova was a passive partner. Possibly, the partners with whom she most often danced were also too passive to rouse her creative temperament. After the premiere of *The Creation of the World,* Kolpakova

TOP. *Eve: Natalia Bolshakova;*
Adam: Vadim Gulyaev.
BOTTOM. *Eve: Bolshakova;*
Adam: Gulyaev; Angel:
Lyudmilla Semenyaka.

frequently danced with Baryshnikov and became noticeably more animated on those occasions.

   The two danced their first love duet with great feeling. The emotional
confusion resulting from Adam and Eve's discovery of love drove them
about the stage, as wind scatters the leaves. Repeatedly, their new feelings united them, flying, and then separated them. In a somber mood,
saddened by the onslaught of the unfamiliar adult emotions, Adam and

75

76

Eve leave the Garden of Eden voluntarily. In the last *pas de deux,* ·after the demise of the Devil and the She-Devil and after Eve's escape from death, Kolpakova conveyed quiet and sublime passion.

Love, the triumph over peril, and the conception of a child with the woman he loved, all raised Baryshnikov's Adam to a new level of spiritual development: he comprehended his responsibility for other people. Even though the choreography of *The Creation of the World* did not provide material for great acting, it still demanded that Baryshnikov portray a character experiencing the entire gamut of human maturation.

In the last section of *The Creation of the World,* all of the characters appeared onstage together, as in a finale. The dancers detached themselves from their roles and parodied the images that they had sustained

Act III. Adam: Baryshnikov.

up to that point. Misha jumped to an incredible height with straight legs and deliberately flexed feet, beating his heels. The audience laughed and applauded. Baryshnikov reminded us of the mischievousness of his Adam and at the same time made light fun of him.

Misha had an unconditional triumph in *The Creation of the World* and furthered the success of the ballet as a whole. However, when Yury Soloviev stopped dancing the role of God, the ballet resembled a lame animal: it was able to run, but one of its legs was obviously less capable than the others.

Before Baryshnikov's emergence, Yury Soloviev was the leading star of the Kirov Ballet. (I do not include Nureyev, since he danced in Leningrad for only a short time.) Soloviev had an irreproachable technique. In his jumps, he had phenomenal *élévation* and a very soft landing; he could easily execute a *double tour en l'air*. But nature, after having endowed Soloviev so generously with all the talents of a leading dancer, sharply limited their use. Both in his external appearance (a solid, stocky figure, with bulging leg muscles, and a plain, inexpressive face) and his acting ability, Soloviev lacked the qualities of a prince. He did not have sufficient talent to overcome the obstacles of his physical and artistic endowments in order to portray romantic roles convincingly. And because there was nothing original in his performances—he simply adapted himself to the traditional notion of a lyrical hero—this lack of inspiration

In the dressing room after the premiere.

reinforced his natural shortcomings. Soloviev was successful in contemporary roles portraying the common man, Danila in *The Stone Flower* and the Youth in *Symphony #7*, but there were not enough of these roles in the theater's repertory to make up a career.

And then, suddenly, he created God! Soloviev revealed a vivid, sharply temperamental side to his character in this role, alternating between humorousness and sorrow. Stocky and round faced, he was God: the Creator, the ceaseless worker, and a mournful slave to his own principles. He was the loving Father, raising his children and then experiencing loss and heartache. Soloviev executed the light *jetés* and the quick, mincing steps of the choreography magnificently. However, Soloviev apparently did not regard his success with any confidence. Perhaps he did not perceive how masterfully he interpreted this role. Perhaps he was resentful that he was not dancing the principal role and that younger artists were already taking his place. Or he may have sincerely believed that the gallant-prince roles were his calling. Soon after the premiere, Soloviev began, under various pretexts, to avoid performing in *The Creation of the World* to the detriment of the production as a whole.

Soloviev's fate was tragic. Outwardly he was a simple, quiet person whose passion in life was fishing. He had a family, which included his wife, Tatyana Legat (from the celebrated family of Russian dancers), a former dancer who today is a coach at the Kirov, and a daughter. Soloviev possessed all of the highest privileges of a Soviet artist, such as participation in all foreign tours of the company. But, on December 1, 1977, Soloviev drove to his dacha and shot himself. He left no note. By all indications, however, he had planned his suicide in advance.

In Leningrad, after Yury's death, many people said that this would have been Misha's fate if he had not stayed in America.

But, for Misha at least, on March 20, 1971—the morning of the preview for *The Creation of the World*—life was still full of hope. Misha had just finished the filming of the television production *Fiesta*, and had before him his debut in *Giselle* and in a new ballet, *The Prince of the Pagodas* by Oleg Vinogradov.

In 1971, we were all still living with illusions, the artist's only basis for hope within Soviet society. There seemed to be a future filled with promise.

FIESTA

T he year 1971 was the peak of Baryshnikov's artistic career in Leningrad. During this period, he not only matured as a ballet dancer but also made his acting debut. He was offered the role of Pedro Romero in *Fiesta*, a feature film made for television, based on Ernest Hemingway's *The Sun Also Rises*.

The production was directed by Sergei Yursky, one of the Soviet Union's outstanding actors. At that time, he was a member of the Bolshoi Dramatic Theater, the leading repertory company in Leningrad. The most accomplished actors of the BDT took part in the film. What induced Yursky to invite Baryshnikov to play a dramatic role? Yursky himself provided an answer to this question in his book *Who Holds the Pause*. "For an actor, the path to the spirit of a character always lies in the body, in movement." Most likely, Yursky cast a ballet dancer in the role of a matador because of the athleticism and grace required of both. The choice of Mikhail Baryshnikov did not provoke any doubts, even that early in his career.

In the final analysis, Baryshnikov's participation in the film was not only a personal triumph, in which he proved himself to be a talented actor, but also a fortunate addition to the entire venture.

Paralleling Hemingway, Yursky staged his film with two epigraphs in mind: Gertrude Stein's remark, "You are all a lost generation"; and the verse from *Ecclesiastes*, "The wind goeth toward the south, and tur-

neth about unto the north; it whirleth about continually, and the wind returneth again according to his circuits." Striving to embody these ideas in a cinematic form and to elucidate the philosophical basis of the work, Yursky began the film by moving all the characters in a circle, in the empty expanse of a film studio.

Initially, the characters are wrapped up in themselves. In their isolation they reveal their true characters, in contrast to their subsequent masked behavior with one another.

Baryshnikov as Romero stood out from the other characters, especially in outward appearance. He alone moved in the erect and well-balanced manner of a ballet dancer. During the rehearsals, which I photographed in the studio, it seemed to me that Baryshnikov felt somewhat constrained in an unfamiliar situation, as a dancer among actors. But when I saw the film, it was evident that Baryshnikov's outward carriage corresponded completely to Romero's place among the other characters in the story. His exterior constraint hid the internal reserve of a matador. Furthermore, even the idiosyncrasies of Baryshnikov's pronunciation were advantageous in creating his character. In the novel, Romero is a Spaniard speaking in English, and Baryshnikov's untrained speech suggested a foreign accent.

Baryshnikov remained dignified in his few scenes with Brett. Yursky almost deprived Romero and Lady Brett Ashley of spontaneous, lifelike contact, most noticeably in their intimate moments. In the scene where they meet, and even in the last one before the bullfight, Brett and Romero hardly look at one another: Brett because she is anxious about her destiny and Romero because what is most important in his life—the bullfight—is still before him.

Baryshnikov's Pedro Romero lives for the *corrida*. He is a participant in the celebration; the remaining characters are only spectators. They are passive; Romero is an active force.

Jake, of course, is the main character, and the story is told from his point of view in the film as in the novel. Jake is distinct from the other idle personalities in the drama; like Pedro, he, too, has his role in life. He is a writer, and the pathetic movement of the characters in a circle, with which the film starts, occurs to the tapping of his typewriter. Like his peers, Jake passively submits to the flow of life, yet he interprets what he sees.

The real triumph for Baryshnikov in his small role was in the last shots before the beginning of the bullfight: the "dressing" of Romero by his retainers and his entrance into the arena. Outwardly calm and collected, and in the white regalia of a matador, he was dressed either for a celebration or for death. A beautiful boy, a great artist, stood entirely alone confronting his singular fate. He entered, paused, and looking straight out at us from the screen, removed his hat, as if to greet us, the viewers, with the regal gesture of a prince.

Perhaps, Yursky had this stunning moment in mind when he invited Baryshnikov to play the part.

Baryshnikov as Pedro Romero.

85

Although it was forbidden to mention Baryshnikov's name in the official press after his defection in 1974, and even more so to show a film in which he appeared, I did see *Fiesta* again in 1977, just before my departure from the Soviet Union. At that time, various professional clubs, the University Club for students, the Theatrical Museum, and the Theatrical Institute suddenly were permitted to show the film to their members. At about this time, a friend of mine told me that he had obtained

ABOVE. *Pedro Romero and Brett meet for the first time. From left to right, Pedro Romero: Baryshnikov; Michael: Mikhail Volkov; Brett: Natalia Tenyakova.* ABOVE RIGHT. *Brett reads Pedro Romero's palm: "There are thousands of bulls."* RIGHT. *Pedro Romero and Brett (Tenyakova).*

FACING PAGE. *Pedro Romero before his entrance into the ring.*

86

Pedro Romero.

and delivered the film to the home of a party official, at her request. The woman's position did not allow her publicly to display interest in a film in which a "traitor to the motherland" played a part, but she desperately wanted to see it.

Who, and for what reason, released *Fiesta* for this semipublic showing? No one knows.

This last time, I saw the film in an almost empty auditorium: the members of one of the professional clubs had taken the opportunity of showing the film and had invited only close friends of members to see it.

So we saw Baryshnikov once again on the pristine white screen. The only change that had been made was the removal of the credits with the names of the actors and the characters they played. The film as a whole appealed to me more than it had in 1971. Perhaps Yursky's melancholy interpretation of the novel corresponded to my own predeparture mood? To what part of the world can we go to escape ourselves? What celebration can compensate for the loss of friends?

All that remains available from this film are photographs and the recollections of those who saw it. The film itself lies locked in a file cabinet somewhere. But, to this day, in one apartment that Misha frequented during the rehearsals of *Fiesta*, there lives a strange, unsociable cat. Sometimes, if pressed—"Osya, show us how Baryshnikov walks"— the cat will withdraw to the end of a dark corridor. Then he will walk toward his audience, proudly thrusting forward his soft paws, turned out into first position.

FACING PAGE. *The last glimpse of Baryshnikov in* Fiesta.

88

GISELLE

A classic is a classic because it is contemporary and eternal.

—Yury Slonimsky, *Giselle*

Albrecht in *Giselle* is now a permanent role in Baryshnikov's repertory. But, on January 5, 1972, he appeared onstage in this part for the first time.

Baryshnikov ran onto the stage in a state of laughter and anxiety. His Albrecht was experiencing the agitations and the joy of love for the first time. He was touchingly young, practically still a boy; he had just fallen in love and was stunned by the feelings he had discovered. Baryshnikov himself was so nervous before his debut in *Giselle* that the anxiety of the artist intensified the feelings of his Albrecht. This nervousness was communicated to us, the viewers; it corresponded to the excitement and the joy in our hearts before the spectacle that we were about to see. Even the rather unflattering costume did not mar Baryshnikov's image. Anyone who was at Baryshnikov's first *Giselle* would agree, I think, that never again would we see such a spontaneously ardent Albrecht, even from Baryshnikov himself. Misha's debut in *Giselle* received rave reviews in the press and provoked a tremendous response from the theater world.

Giselle has always been one of the Russian public's favorite classical ballets. This is probably not only because the choreography by Jules Perrot and Marius Petipa is so utterly beautiful, but also because the story provides, as Yury Slonimsky wrote, "a sublime drama of the heart."

To recount the plot of the ballet briefly, the young Count Albrecht falls in love with a simple peasant girl, Giselle, whom he cannot marry because of their difference in class. He is already engaged to Bathilde, the daughter of a duke. Giselle is not aware of the exalted origin of her beloved, and when the truth is revealed, Giselle dies of a broken heart. The Count, filled with repentance, goes at night to the cemetery where Giselle is buried. The Wilis, girls who died before marrying, come out of their graves and kill every man they meet. Among the Wilis is Giselle. Albrecht begs her forgiveness; Giselle in turn begs the Wilis to spare Albrecht. The Wilis are unmoved, but then the sun begins to rise and they disappear. Giselle, who has forgiven Albrecht, also disappears. The outline of the story is very spare; the rest of the drama depends on the performers.

A large body of written and oral recollections has accumulated in Russia about the performances of great dancers of the past in *Giselle*. My generation of ballet audiences, for example, remembers Galina Ulanova well. Thus, balletomanes greet every debut in *Giselle* with enormous, albeit highly critical, interest. For a dancer, an appearance in *Giselle* is not only a crucial examination of his or her technical skill, but also of the dancer's independence in dramatic interpretation. After World War II, when Ulanova joined the Bolshoi Ballet in Moscow, Natalia Dudinskaya and Konstantin Sergeyev emerged as the principal interpreters of *Giselle* on the Leningrad stage. During their era, the ballet looked like a stiff and lifeless museum piece. But in the beginning of the sixties, so many young dancers began to emerge that it became difficult for the older stars to retain their exclusive monopoly of *Giselle*. One after another, Irina Kolpakova, and the even younger Natalia Makarova, Alla Sizova, and Yelena Yevteyeva made their debuts in the role of Giselle. With their various talents, the new dancers demolished the thoroughly icy image of Dudinskaya's Giselle. But it was the men who, in revising the image of Albrecht, provoked the contemporary reading of the ballet.

In Russian dramatic theater it is a tradition to stage classical plays from a contemporary point of view and thus load onto a Hamlet or a Prince Myshkin's shoulders the concerns of the current times. In Soviet ballet theater, the lack of good, contemporary ballets is always felt. From

FACING PAGE. *Baryshnikov made his debut in the role of Albrecht on January 5, 1972.*

year to year, the basis of the repertory consists of the same ballets from the past. Thus, the responsibility for the continual renewal of the classical forms falls on the dancer.

In the twenties, after the revolution, the Leningrad *premier danseur* Boris Shavrov submitted to the ideas of his time. He emphasized the theme of social conflict in *Giselle*. Since the new regime in Russia had declared all representatives of the ruling classes "enemies of the people," Shavrov depicted Count Albrecht as a deceiver, a scoundrel, and a calculating seducer of a poor peasant girl. Konstantin Sergeyev imitated Shavrov's interpretation, but in diluted form, and his Albrecht acquired a more romantic coloring over the years. When I began to attend the ballet, in the beginning of the fifties, Sergeyev was at the end of his career, a dancer who had lost his ballet technique and a lyrical hero who had lost the capability for romantic emotions. He sobbed timorously on the shoulder of his Friend at the end of the first act and in the second act he was occupied with the technical difficulties of the *adagio*.

Misha told me in Leningrad that the most interesting Albrecht he had seen at the Kirov was that of Svyatoslav Kuznetsov. Kuznetsov was one of the most talented artists of the "lost generation" of Soviet ballet theater. This generation came to the stage during the period of drama ballet's decline at the end of the forties and the beginning of the fifties. Unfortunately for Kuznetsov, he was the constant understudy of Sergeyev. Because of this, he became firmly established as the "successor" of the aging star. But, in fact, Kuznetsov was always distinctly original and independent in his portrayal of Albrecht. Of course, he had to follow Sergeyev's interpretation in certain respects, simply because of the libretto. But Sergeyev's concept of social conflict did not enter into Kuznetsov's interpretation. His Albrecht did not deceive Giselle consciously; he was simply infatuated with a young girl who naïvely took his infatuation for love. He followed the path from sensual passion to spiritual love, because he had a sincere and noble heart. Kuznetsov was the first dancer in Leningrad to shift the accent of this drama from Giselle to Albrecht. He danced the second act as if he truly saw an apparition; he compelled the audience to believe that Giselle appeared only in Albrecht's imagination.

Kuznetsov matured as an artist during the postwar period and the

FACING PAGE. *Ninel Petrova and Svyatoslav Kuznetsov in the second act of* Giselle. *1958.*

95

Natalia Makarova and Nikita Dolgushin in the second act of Giselle. 1968.

end of the Stalinist era. He upheld the ideal of beauty onstage as if to counter the destructive era of wars and revolutions. His heroes were handsome and sublimely romantic. Even his Iago (in the ballet *Othello*, with music by Aleksey Machavariani and choreography by Vakhtang Chabukiani) was not simply a scheming or envious man but an unsuccessful Napoleon. Moreover, Kuznetsov's heroes were tragically lonely.

But the young artists who came to the stage at the very end of the fifties and the beginning of the sixties were not concerned with social problems; they had grown up in a more or less stable society and came of age at the moment of relative, temporary liberalization under Khrushchev. The times had changed and the tastes of the audience had also changed subtly. The new generation of actors brought the problems of their era to the stage. They were much more aware of the world at large than their predecessors had been; they were akin to their peers in Europe. In addition, these young dancers restored male dancing to its former brilliance, which had been lost during the ascendancy of drama ballet. They even expanded its technical possibilities to limits beyond anything achieved by the dancers of drama ballet or the virtuosos of the past. The new dancers fundamentally altered the image of Albrecht.

I did not see Nureyev dance Albrecht, but the reaction to his appearance in *Giselle* was enormous. The new life of an old ballet began with Nureyev and continued with Natalia Makarova and Nikita Dolgushin, who made their debuts at the same time. These young dancers, in particular, shifted the conflict of the story from the realm of class struggle to that of morality. Dolgushin's Albrecht was outwardly a nobleman. Unlike Sergeyev's, his Albrecht was not a perfidious seducer, but, rather, an aristocrat and a philosopher. He was not passionately in love. Portraying a genuine Petersburg intellectual, Dolgushin's Albrecht was too refined to abandon himself to heartfelt impulses. He was not cold but he was restrained in his feeling. However, in the second act, he was uniquely romantic, and sad, especially with Natalia Makarova as Giselle. Suffering and the feeling of guilt gave birth to the poet in him. Parted from Giselle forever, Dolgushin's Albrecht suddenly drew himself up and walked directly downstage toward the audience, spreading his arms and raising them in an expressive movement, as if to reveal his innermost self. He converted his guilt and the death of Giselle into a poetic soliloquy and thus found his path to redemption.

From Baryshnikov's first moment onstage in this role, he rejected the path of all other Albrechts, which led from a simple infatuation to the realization of love. From the very beginning of the ballet, he maintained a high level of emotional tension. The entire ballet, right up to the appearance of the Count and Albrecht's fiancée, revolved around his immersion in an unrestrained love duet—making the collision of the idyll with real life all the more terrible.

In Leningrad, the role of Bathilde, Albrecht's bride, is traditionally played by a beautiful, but older, dancer. Baryshnikov, during his preparation for the ballet, commented, "It is wrong that Bathilde in our production is always older than Albrecht. Albrecht should turn around to face his bride and before him there is a young girl. One just like Giselle." Thus the moral conflict of the ballet would lie in the choice between the two young girls. Albrecht was not deceiving either Bathilde or Giselle. While falling in love with Giselle, he simply forgot about the existence of the rest of the world. As a result, he transgressed his previously existing and heartfelt commitment to his fiancée. And so the day of reckoning arrived: for Giselle—death; for Bathilde—misery; for Albrecht—despair, the loss of his beloved, and overwhelming guilt.

I always watch the interpreter of Albrecht attentively at the moment

when he collides face to face with his bride and she asks him the natural question, "What does all of this mean?"

Kuznetsov proffered his hand to his fiancée as etiquette would demand. He led Bathilde downstage with a frozen expression on his face. His hero hoped that the ambiguous gesture of his arm around his head, which signified, "It is just my fantasy," would be sufficient explanation for his peasant attire and his actions. He hated any clarifications of relationships or any female hysterics, whether Bathilde's or Giselle's. When Giselle flung herself at him, grabbing him by the shoulders and trying to read the truth in his eyes, he turned his head away and transformed himself into a stone sculpture.

Dolgushin proffered his hand to his fiancée with the gesture of a refined young man who had not yet entirely comprehended his position. Baryshnikov submitted to Bathilde in total confusion upon seeing people

FACING PAGE, TOP LEFT, TOP RIGHT, AND BOTTOM. *Alla Sizova and Mikhail Baryshnikov in the first act of* Giselle. *January 5, 1972.*

Albrecht: Baryshnikov. His first performance of Giselle. *January 5, 1972.*

about whom he had completely forgotten. He mechanically walked alongside Bathilde, not hearing her question. His glance was turned inward to his own soul: his reckoning began at that moment.

Baryshnikov did not give his Friend the opportunity to lead him away from the body of the dead Giselle. He went down on his knees at her feet, and, at the last moment, he collapsed, falling toward the corpse as if awaiting celestial punishment for causing another's death. But the retribution did not yet begin.

Baryshnikov entered in the second act to the mournful strains of the oboe. The first time I watched him from the audience, I felt my heart break—his Albrecht conveyed such tension and anguish. There were neither impetuous pirouettes nor brilliant jumps in this entrance; none of the pyrotechnics with which Baryshnikov captivated his audiences in other ballets. He simply appeared onstage in a cloak and hat, flowers in his arms. He paced downstage along a diagonal toward Giselle's grave. Then, with the *manège* that occurs after Albrecht catches sight of Giselle, Baryshnikov stunned everyone. During this series of leaps, by a movement of his wrists, he created the impression of a constrained cry of despair escaping from his breast. He was a tormented soul flying in a circle, his hands flailing in the dark. Then, his anguish spent, he sank to his knees and became still. Throughout the second act Baryshnikov built the drama, alternating the relative smoothness of the *adagio* with the impetuous outcries of the soul. Thus, for example, Baryshnikov abruptly ended the *brisés,* which Albrecht executes in a diagonal across the stage in *renversé* on high *demi-pointe,* again creating the illusion of a cry of mental agony. Throughout the *adagio* in the second act, he presented, like Kuznetsov, a dialogue with a phantom of his imagination. But he called Giselle to this illusory meeting neither to beg forgiveness nor to make a declaration of love. He had to see her, whether in reality or in delirium. He did not beg forgiveness because no one could have forgiven him. Neither Giselle, nor God, nor anyone else could absolve him of his guilt, since he did not forgive himself. Thus Baryshnikov resolved the moral question of responsibility for evil. Each person was meant to bear the responsibility for all the harm and suffering he caused, whether accidental or not. Only his own conscience would judge him and there would be no acquittal before that judge.

LEFT. *Sizova and Baryshnikov in the January 5, 1972, performance.* BELOW AND FOLLOWING PAGE. *The second act.*

Baryshnikov danced *Giselle* in Leningrad for almost three entire seasons. During this period, as he changed, his Albrecht changed, although the basic interpretation of the role remained the same. Gradually, he stopped expressing his love for Giselle in the first act so spontaneously and passionately; the youthful impulsiveness disappeared. But the more bitterness accumulated in Baryshnikov's life, the more tragic his image of Albrecht became in the second act. I vividly remember his last performance of *Giselle* at the Kirov Theater on April 30, 1974. At the very end of the ballet, when Giselle was being lowered into the grave, Baryshnikov suddenly threw his head back in a desperate gesture. Usually, in the Kirov production, the dawn begins at that moment. However, on this occasion it seemed to me that the stage was plunged into even greater darkness. Albrecht looked heavenward into a black void. He rose from his knees and began to withdraw, scattering the flowers he held in his hands. In the middle of the stage he suddenly fell, holding his hands toward the grave like a man whose mental powers have abandoned him forever. Between Albrecht and Giselle's grave a path of flowers remained. The curtain closed. A sensation of horror before this terrifying, hopeless ending remained with me.

Later, in Paris, in the spring of 1979, I recalled this performance when I saw Baryshnikov dance Hermann in Roland Petit's ballet *La Dame de Pique* (to the music of Tchaikovsky). Here, the submergence of an exhausted human being in darkness was the conscious solution of the role. But when Baryshnikov first employed this image, in that last performance of *Giselle* in Leningrad, it was involuntary, the first awakening of an emotion, one month before the tour to Canada.

In a conversation in New York, I asked Baryshnikov how he had pictured his artistic future then, before his departure.

"I didn't," he answered. There was no future. Before Baryshnikov in April 1974 there was only darkness.

But Baryshnikov first danced *Giselle* during a time of creative ascent for him. His first Giselle was Alla Sizova, a sweet, ingenuous creature. In the second act, she was captivating not only in her beautiful lines and in the seeming weightlessness of her dancing, but also in her touching defenselessness. However, she made no contact with Misha onstage. He always complained that all he ever saw were her empty eyes. Sizova did not change in her performances, whether she danced with Baryshnikov or with another partner. Purely in terms of external appearance, the cool but more modern Yelena Yevteyeva was more suited to Baryshnikov in *Giselle,* especially in the second act.

Nevertheless, the lack of an equally talented partner remained one of the essential problems of Misha's professional career in Leningrad. Misha was seeking both a partner for the dance and a truly talented actress, someone with whom it would be satisfying to work. He was interested not only in the results of his own work but also in the impact of the performance as a whole. Like all artists, Misha strove for personal success, but he would have preferred to dance with challenging partners. I believe that Misha preferred being an equal among great talents rather than the first among mediocrities. Probably for these reasons he decided to dance with Natalia Bessmertnova of Moscow, the greatest Giselle of that time.

Bessmertnova was a unique ballerina, totally unlike her peers both in Moscow and in Leningrad. Tall, thin, with enormous eyes and beautiful wrists, she interpreted Giselle as if she had been born to dance the role. Especially good in the second act, she also excelled in the first. She did not imitate the traditional image by playing a little girl in the usual artificial style. From her first entrance until her disappearance into the grave, she was herself. The emotions she provoked are indescribable. In the winter of 1972, when Baryshnikov was invited to appear in a televised performance of the second act of *Giselle,* he asked Bessmertnova to dance with him. In the Soviet Union it was not customary for an artist to choose his own partner. This act on Misha's part was a manifestation of his recurrent audacity in challenging the established order. As a result of his choice, an amusing series of events occurred.

A taped version was to be made in the afternoon and, in the evening, the *adagio* was to be performed and broadcast live. Arriving just before eleven o'clock in the morning at one of the studios in the TV station to watch the rehearsal, I found Misha in a somewhat agitated state. Instead of greeting me he said, "I have resigned from the theater."

As it turned out, Misha had gone to the administrative director of the Kirov Theater, Petr Rachinsky, earlier that morning to request permission to rehearse with Bessmertnova in a room in the theater. Ra-

TOP, MIDDLE, BOTTOM.
*The Wilis. The beginning
of the second act of*
Giselle.

chinsky not only refused, but also added, "I forbid you to film *Giselle* with Bessmertnova. We have plenty of our own ballerinas in the theater. Aren't they good enough?"

Petr Rachinsky, a man of simple, "proletarian" origin who understood nothing about art, and who was rumored to have been a fireman prior to his appointment as director, apparently was placed at the head of one of the most prominent ballet companies in the Soviet Union precisely because of his total lack of qualifications. The Soviet cultural authorities felt that, as a longtime party worker with a good reputation, he would be able to provide ideological party leadership at the Kirov.

In all theaters in the Soviet Union, a reliable party member supervises the actual management; the less intelligent the person is and the less he understands art, the better. In important institutions such as the Kirov, where the troupe travels abroad, one of the subordinate administrators (Rachinsky had two) is a KGB worker or at least a direct link from the company to the KGB. The head of the personnel department, or "first department," in all theaters is *always* closely connected with either a KGB collaborator or employee. The personnel department, in addition to hiring theater employees, records not only everyone's place of birth and other ordinary biographical data but also every bit of information that might be of future interest to the KGB.

The artistic director is occupied with creative matters. But the extent of his control often depends on the administrative director, and the character of each participant plays a large role in the actual distribution of power in the theater. Petr Rachinsky was a powerful, despotic personality who steadfastly believed that he understood the problems of ballet perfectly, and certainly no less than professionals. According to the artists, at a meeting of the *artsoviet*—or artistic council—he once said, "Why do I need a ballet master? I myself know who should be assigned to dance the little swans."

An *artsoviet* exists in every theater and creates the outward appearance of democratic leadership. It consists of party representatives within the theater, members of the trade unions, the artistic director and assistant ballet masters, the leading artists, and the so-called friends of the theater: critics, composers, and others. Members of the *artsoviet* meet to discuss possible new works, to listen to new music, and to approve

FACING PAGE, TOP. *Yelena Yevteyeva and Baryshnikov. 1972–1973.* BOTTOM LEFT AND RIGHT. *Alla Sizova and Baryshnikov. 1973.*

107

Albrecht.

Irina Kolpakova, Baryshnikov.
1973.

RIGHT. *The Fiancée: Lelya*
Petrova. Albrecht: Baryshnikov.
FACING PAGE. *Albrecht.*

The end of the first act.

new ballets before the premiere takes place.

Whether Rachinsky actually made such a remark—or if artists who detested him simply thought it up—it accurately reflects his manner of thinking and his style of behavior. Rachinsky regarded his theater as a landowner would have perceived his property in former times; he practically considered the artists serfs. He was so accustomed to the obedience of his fearful troupe that it did not even occur to him that a young dancer might have the courage to disobey him. But Misha was not a slave. He always defended his position when the matter concerned his creative work.

Misha wrote his declaration of resignation from the Kirov, put it on the secretary's desk, and left the theater to rehearse with Bessmertnova. The story spread instantly. In the middle of the day, several ballet dancers engaged in other broadcasts arrived at the television station. Their reaction was paradoxical: many of them censured Misha. Intimidated, accustomed to obeying a hated director, these people could not forgive Misha for *not* feeling threatened by Rachinsky and for defying his despotism. He had acted as not one of them would have dared.

110

Some of the other dancers even avoided him at this time. During a break between takes, Misha and I walked along a corridor. Another principal dancer from the Kirov approached us, cheerfully swinging a red cloak that was part of his costume. Misha did not notice him, but he noticed us. He paused for a second and then, perhaps not knowing how to respond to the situation, disappeared; it was as if he had slipped through the wall. Unsure how Rachinsky would react to Misha's challenge, he had apparently decided to be on the safe side, and not associate himself with the scandal. Misha and he had always had a friendly rapport; yet the psychology of fearful, entangled Soviet citizens is often baffling. This same dancer, who was not a friend of mine, telephoned me on the eve of my departure from the Soviet Union. Although aware that my telephone was tapped, he nevertheless identified himself and then wished me a good trip. But in the TV station corridor, he had lost his head. He did not know what consequences Misha would suffer as a result of his audacious action, and it is likely that he did not want to jeopardize his own chances of being included in the upcoming tour to Spain by associating with Misha.

There is not a more unhappy or morally corrupt group than a collective of Soviet ballet artists before a foreign tour. Many of the dancers write denunciations of their colleagues, and of the stars in particular, which they submit to the director. They attempt to stress their own "loyal" feelings by asserting that they know of another artist's desire to remain abroad. Those who are not chosen to go on tour consider themselves insulted and unfortunate, interpreting their exclusion as an indication of second-class citizenship. The authorities understand the enticement of a foreign tour perfectly well and use it adeptly at necessary moments. Valery Panov had submitted an application to emigrate to Israel early in 1972. Soon afterward, a meeting was held to encourage the artists to condemn Panov for "betrayal of the motherland." The timing was calculated precisely: the company was preparing for the tour to Spain. Who among them did not want to see Madrid? Who did not want to see the paintings by Goya, or buy Western shoes, or just get out from behind the iron curtain and see the world? Practically everyone had reason to fear that if he did not come out against Panov, he would not be taken abroad. Hence, many dancers discredited the "traitor," even some who occupied secure enough positions to have enabled them to

FOLLOWING PAGES.
*Baryshnikov at the beginning
of the second act.*

111

remain silent. However, there were a few steadfast and decent people who did not participate. Baryshnikov did not go to the meeting. Yury Soloviev refused to speak out against Panov. Vazira Ganibalova, a ballerina in the company, listened at length to the condemnations. Finally she picked up her towel, an indispensable accessory for a dancer, and said, "Well, you can sit here and talk, but I am going to work. I have a performance coming up soon." I don't remember whether or not Ganibalova and Soloviev went to Spain, but Baryshnikov did go. Even if Misha had not, he would not have repented of his own action. Nothing could compel him to forget his human dignity.

Thus Baryshnikov submitted his resignation from the theater and left to work with Bessmertnova. They spent the entire day in the television

Albrecht.

studio, rehearsing the *adagio* during the morning, making the taped version in the afternoon, and performing the live broadcast that evening.

The real-life drama played itself out quickly. Baryshnikov was called to the theater the following morning. Rachinsky gently scolded him, "What were you in such a rush for? I didn't want you to do anything of the sort." The resignation was refused. The ballet world, however, instantly created another version of this story, which went as follows: Rachinsky went to Leningrad's highest cultural authorities with Misha's resignation to ask how he should respond. He was told that he could accept Baryshnikov's resignation from the Kirov but, along with it, he would be asked to submit his own, which his superiors would likewise accept. Early the following morning, two of Rachinsky's secretaries arrived at Misha's apartment in a black *Volga* limousine, the Soviet equivalent of a Cadillac. After dragging Misha out of bed by the arms, they

drove him to the theater. Rachinsky was waiting at the entrance with outstretched arms and greeted Misha reproachfully but affectionately, "What's the matter with you, Misha! Why, I love you like my own son!" Rachinsky did not sign Misha's resignation, and the drama ended quickly. I do not know if the party chiefs actually comprehended the value of Baryshnikov's talent or if they feared losing a *valyutnyi*, or "hard currency" dancer. (Western impresarios will pay the Soviet government well for tours in which certain artists are included—hence the slang expression—and Misha was one of these artists.)

I do not know what became of the film of *Giselle*, made during the winter of 1972. Some people said that, by order of party officials, Misha's image was "washed away" the day after he defected. Others said that quick-witted workers in the television studio managed to take the film home. I have kept my photographs.

*Baryshnikov at the end
of a performance.*

RIGHT, BELOW TOP. *Morning rehearsal at the TV studio.* Adagio *from the second act of* Giselle. BELOW BOTTOM. *Natalia Bessmertnova in rehearsal. For television.*

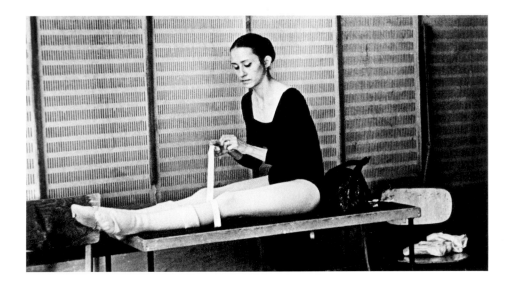

TOP LEFT, LEFT, AND
ABOVE. *Rehearsal before the
television shoot.*

121

Baryshnikov before the beginning of the filming.

BELOW AND FOLLOWING PAGES. *Bessmertnova and Baryshnikov*. Adagio *from the second act of* Giselle.

NOSTALGIA

---

*I lost the sense of reality: in the world opening up before
me there was no perspective.*

—Aleksander Grin, *The Shining World*

During seven years of work in the Soviet Union, Misha danced fifteen to sixteen parts, including *pas de deux* and *pas de trois*. Of these ballets, he danced regularly in only three: *Don Quixote, The Creation of the World*, and *Giselle*. In comparison, a dancer in the West may learn four to six works in one season alone.

After Misha's debut in *Giselle* on January 5, 1972, a year went by before his next opportunity to appear in a work that was new for him. Oleg Vinogradov staged a version of Benjamin Britten's ballet *The Prince of the Pagodas,* in which Misha created the leading role. No one has ever managed to stage an interesting production of this work by Britten, and neither did Vinogradov. The premiere took place on December 30, 1972; altogether, the ballet was performed only three or four times. I did not like Misha's work in this ballet, although Vinogradov did stage one truly effective moment in which Misha as Salamander slithers out of a fire. After Salamander's transformation into a prince, Misha appeared in a traditional, classical *adagio*. The awkward choreography and the unattractive costumes did not emphasize any of Misha's finer qualities; he seemed stocky and lacked charm. Half a year of work and a season had been wasted. And Misha was at the prime of his life, his technical and creative abilities seemingly boundless. He dreamed only of having new work.

The summer of 1972 provided my last recollections of a cheerful and carefree Misha. Misha and his puppy, Foma, my close friend Lena and her husband and daughter, my mother, my two children, and I all shared a country house. (Tanya Koltsova had gone to visit her mother in another city.) The dacha was located on the Karelian Isthmus, the peninsula Finland ceded to the USSR during World War II. The climate is normally severe, but that summer it was uncommonly hot, so we swam a great deal. We were happy and relaxed. Misha allowed himself to slip out of shape completely. Lena's husband taught the older children archery with a bow that he had made from the branch of a juniper. My six-month-old daughter, Masha, sat outside all day long on the lawn, chatting with the birds. During the evenings when it became cool, we would go down to the lake and sit on the shore. Lena would sing old Russian songs that her grandmother had taught her. "The Rivulet Palenga" was particularly popular with us: "Hello, rivulet Palenga, little gold mine. . . . From it Alenka and I parted to opposite sides, to opposite sides." As the scarlet streaks of the sunset slowly faded, the lake became submerged in mist.

At the end of August, we returned to Leningrad. That September, our friend Sasha Minz emigrated to the West. He had become anxious while waiting for his visa; the unknown future both excited and scared him.

I was not able to see Sasha on the night before his departure. I had just separated from my husband and had no one to stay with little Masha. But Misha went to see Sasha off. This act on Misha's part was a direct challenge to the authorities. Such unconcealed sympathy toward an emigrant is perceived as a manifestation of political unreliability.

Despite the fact that his mother, who went with him, was terminally ill, Sasha did not lose his good humor. While working with La Scala Ballet in Milan, he wrote me cheerful postcards. And he invariably asked, "How is the Little Prince doing?" It must have been Sasha who gave Misha that nickname.

But the Little Prince was becoming increasingly gloomy. Occasionally

ABOVE AND LEFT. *Misha at the dacha. Summer 1972.*

Misha's first performance as Désiré in The Sleeping Beauty. *Act II: the Hunt Scene. June 21, 1970.*

ABOVE RIGHT. *The Lilac Fairy: Alla Osipenko. Prince Désiré: Baryshnikov. First performance.* **RIGHT.** *Aurora: Alla Sizova; Prince Désiré: Baryshnikov. First performance.*

such bouts of melancholy and hopeless depression would descend upon him that he would call me, or other friends of his, and say, "I feel horrible; please come visit me."

There was no work in the theater and no prospects for new work. After the failure of *The Prince of the Pagodas,* it seemed that the Kirov Ballet had died completely. In October 1972, after an interval of almost two years, Misha again danced Prince Désiré (as Florimund is known in the USSR) in *The Sleeping Beauty.* Misha did not make a great impression on me in that performance. Désiré, whose function is that of an elegant cavalier, is the most "abstract" hero of all of the leading roles in the great classical ballets. In general, characterless parts are the least successful roles in Baryshnikov's repertory. Although Misha once said to me that he becomes tired of interpreting parts, it is interpretation that is one of the strongest aspects of Baryshnikov's artistic gift.

But Baryshnikov made a tremendous impression as Désiré when he danced this role in Leningrad for the last time, in 1973. Misha danced the hunt scene romantically and mournfully, wrapped up in himself. He preserved this condition of spiritual isolation and poeticism in the classical *adagio* of the fourth act.

A major event occurred in the theatrical life of Leningrad during 1972 with the arrival of George Balanchine's New York City Ballet. The presence of any Western ballet company in the Soviet Union generates great excitement among all of the artists and admirers of the ballet: finally we have the chance to see what is happening in ballet elsewhere. Naturally, Misha saw all of Balanchine's and Robbins's programs. During the course of City Ballet's visit, he noticed one very young dancer. "If only I had such a partner!" The dancer was Gelsey Kirkland.

Roland Petit's Les Ballets de Marseilles came to Leningrad twice during Baryshnikov's career. In Paris, in 1978, I read an interview with Petit in which he stated that he had seen Baryshnikov in class during one of the tours and had immediately realized that he was observing a genius. At the time of Petit's visits to Leningrad, he and Misha began to discuss the possibility of working together. Petit wanted to stage a ballet in Leningrad for Baryshnikov, on a Russian theme. However, the Ministry of Culture refused his offer. This collaborative work was finally realized in Paris in 1978, when Roland Petit created a ballet to the music

RIGHT. *Baryshnikov as Désiré in the Hunt Scene. The last performance in* The Sleeping Beauty. *October 6, 1973.*

BELOW AND FACING PAGE, BOTTOM. *Aurora: Irina Kolpakova; Désiré: Baryshnikov. The last performance.*

ABOVE. *Svetlana Yefremova and Baryshnikov dancing the* pas de deux *from* Don Quixote *on* TV.

of the Russian composer Petr Tchaikovsky, on the theme of the story "The Queen of Spades" by the Russian poet Aleksandr Pushkin, for a renegade Russian dancer, Mikhail Baryshnikov. In my opinion, *The Queen of Spades* is the finest ballet that has been created for Baryshnikov in the West.

During the 1972–1973 season, Baryshnikov appeared on television in several excerpts from classical ballets. He danced the *pas de deux* from *Don Quixote* with Svetlana Yefremova, the *adagio* from *The Sleeping Beauty* with Irina Kolpakova, the *adagio* from *Giselle* with Natalia Bessmertnova, and the white *adagio* in Act II from *Swan Lake* with Lyudmilla Putinova, a soloist from Leonid Yakobson's Choreographic Miniatures Ensemble.

By the end of 1972 Misha's relationship with Tanya had begun to deteriorate. There was no new work in sight for Misha at the theater. On New Year's Eve, Misha, Tanya, Slava Santnaneev, Lena, her husband, and I gathered in my apartment. It was a cheerless occasion. Tanya's manner was icy. Rats crawled out from under the floor in my apartment. Thus began 1973.

Misha and Tanya broke up and got back together several times. Shortly after they had finally decided to get married officially, they separated permanently. At this time, Misha exchanged his apartment for a larger one. In the spring of 1973, Misha moved in, but without Tanya.

During the last years of his life in the Soviet Union, Misha made many new friends among scholars, writers, and dramatic actors. Misha's friends admired him for his intelligence and education—rare qualities among ballet dancers—for his immense talent, and his clearly exceptional qualities as a human being.

Misha frequented my home with a famous and talented Soviet poet and his beautiful wife. The poet was not familiar with the ballet and did not particularly care for it. But he loved Misha as a friend. A person of great gifts, and with a tender heart, he sensed in Misha a kindred spirit. At a small celebration of Misha's last birthday in Leningrad on January 27, 1974, the poet read a wonderful new poem and presented it to Misha. Of the friends who were at this last birthday party, which was one of the last gatherings of Baryshnikov's friends who were not involved in ballet, two besides myself have since emigrated: Slava Santnaneev and our charming friend, a doctor named Kira Braynina.

FACING PAGE. *Baryshnikov dancing the variation from* Don Quixote *on television.*

138

We sat, joked, and talked about both theatrical and nontheatrical problems. The poet read his verses. In Russia, everyone loves to carry on long, intimate conversations, especially in the kitchen, and often until dawn. It is not idle chatter at all. Closed off from the world, we invest massive amounts of emotional energy, intellect, talent, knowledge, and heartfelt kindness in these personal discussions. In many circles in Leningrad, friendship is the only belief, the only means of opposition to the regime. It is not necessary for us to go to see psychiatrists in order to retain our mental equilibrium. We have friends.

During the seventies, many *samizdat* works (self-published works prohibited by the government) were passed from hand to hand. Among the *samizdat* were political books, such as Solzhenitsyn's, and poetry that had no relation to politics but had been prohibited from publication. The poetry was simply the verses that the poets had written as they wished, rather than as they were ordered. After endless mocking, the Soviet government finally exiled poet Joseph Brodsky, who today is considered one of the finest poets of our time. Before his exile, his poetry was passed from hand to hand. One courageous professional reader even recited one of Brodsky's poems in public, although he did not identify the author, and as a result got himself into great trouble.

All of this made us increasingly sad. The older we became, the more we sensed the severity of the dismal Soviet regime. In intellectual circles, the discussions centered on the problems of emigration, politics, and the Soviet positions toward the West. One friend of mine sadly quipped, "The West is different from the Soviet Union because in the West everything is allowed except that which is forbidden, but here everything is forbidden except that which is allowed." However, not everything about the West was comprehensible. What was it like in that paradise on earth? What elements of truth were there in the Soviet propaganda describing the "horrors of capitalism?" We knew that somewhere in the "decaying" West, Brodsky was writing his mournful poetry and the stage careers of Makarova and Nureyev were developing brilliantly.

But Misha was dancing only the same ballets. *Giselle, The Creation of the World,* and *Don Quixote,* and in alternation with other dancers. And time was passing. The love of the closest, dearest, and brightest friends could not replace creative work.

FACING PAGE AND FOLLOWING PAGES. *Irina Kolpakova and Baryshnikov dancing the* adagio *from Act III of* The Sleeping Beauty *on television.*

141

Then, suddenly, the cultural officials started to worry. Even they comprehended that the condition of the ballet in the Kirov Theater was disastrous. There were no premieres of new works planned and the amounts of money that had been spent on each successive failure were not trifling. The theater was not fulfilling its plan. Every Soviet institution, theaters included, has a plan stating what its production must be for one year. The Kirov Ballet was obligated to present two premieres a year, which it often did not succeed in doing.

Finally, in 1973, the authorities abolished the committee for artistic management that had been formed after Sergeyev's dismissal. (Rachinsky, the administrative director, was dismissed from his post later—not because of his poor work, but for his participation in some illegal currency operations. He was removed without a scandal and quietly retired to collect his pension.) Igor Belsky, the artistic director of ballet at the Maly Opera in Leningrad, was appointed to the Kirov. If only this ap-

pointment had been made in 1959, when Igor Belsky, a brilliant character dancer still full of energy and ideas, was staging *The Shore of Hope* with the help of supporters and like-minded people. But by 1973 the company's morale had been broken by lengthy idleness. A ballet critic told me that once, as he walked down an empty corridor while all of the dancers were attending morning classes, he noticed one of the principal dancers aimlessly strolling along.

"Why aren't you in class?" he asked with astonishment.

"What for?" answered the dancer. "My salary is paid all the same." In truth the principal longed for new work, but his joke precisely reflected the attitude of many of the Kirov's artists at that time.

Igor Belsky joined the Kirov in the spring of 1973, but he did not rush into his choreographic duties. (I think that he was afraid of failing, of proving to be past his prime and bankrupt of new ideas, which, in fact, turned out to be the case.) While Belsky was slowly familiarizing

himself with the theater, Baryshnikov received permission to prepare his own "creative evening." Finally, Baryshnikov had new work, and the Kirov was fulfilling its yearly plan.

Thus the 1973–1974 season began with much excitement in the theater: Belsky's arrival inspired vague hopes, and the preparation of a creative evening promised interesting work. Misha cheered up and became utterly absorbed in his work. In the program for his evening he included two ballets by Mai Murdmaa, the artistic director of the Estonia Theater: *Daphnis and Chloë* to Ravel's music and *The Prodigal Son* to Prokofiev. The absence of the customary classical *pas de deux* from the program shocked the conservative people in the theater. Where was *Don Quixote* or the *pas de deux* from *Le Corsaire,* or even the variation from *La Bayadère?*

Misha had begun to work with artist Svetlana Dmitrieva on the sets and costumes during the preceding summer. Belsky, who ardently supported Misha's work, Misha, and I went to Tallin in Estonia. We saw the ballet *The Prodigal Son* at the Estonia Theater. All of us liked the ballet. But *The Prodigal Son* (reworked by Murdmaa for Misha), which I later saw at the Kirov Theater, supplanted the impression of the Tallin version.

FACING PAGE. *Baryshnikov dancing the* adagio *from* Swan Lake *with Lyudmilla Putinova on television. She was a soloist with Leonid Yakobson's Choreographic Miniatures Ensemble.*
LEFT. *Tatyana Koltsova on Rossi Street near the Vaganova Institute. 1972.*

147

FACING PAGE, TOP. *Kira Braynina*. FACING PAGE, BOTTOM. *Mikhail Baryshnikov and Igor Belsky, artistic director of the Kirov Ballet, window shopping in Tallin.* BELOW. *Baryshnikov on a street in Tallin.*

REHEARSALS

*You can never step into the same river twice. But through the dense water
you can make out the river bottom covered with tin cans. And behind
magnificent theatrical decorations you can learn to see the brick wall,
the ropes, the fire extinguisher, and the drunken stagehands.
All this is well known to anyone who has been behind
the wings, even if only once. . . .*

—Sergei Dovlatov, *Compromise*

T he rehearsals for the creative evening began in the fall of
1973. Misha selected his partners with painstaking care.
He worried about the success of the entire evening, which
did not depend on him alone. Misha was striving to create
a program of ballets that would be interesting in all aspects. Gogi Aleksidze began to rehearse his *Ballet Divertissement* to music by Mozart with
Irina Kolpakova in the leading female role. Misha invited Kolpakova and
two young dancers, Tanya Koltsova and Yelena Kondratenko, to dance
the role of Chloë in the ballet *Daphnis and Chloë*. But the *pièce de ré-
sistance* of Misha's evening was to cast Alla Osipenko, who left the Kirov
in 1971, as the Siren in *The Prodigal Son*. Again, Misha openly challenged the theater's administration by inviting her to participate in his
evening. By this time Misha was famous and occupied a prominent position in the theater. The Kirov found itself in such an indisputably bad
situation that the administration had to yield to him in everything. *151*

Baryshnikov in the rehearsal studio. To the left in the mirror: Nina Alovert taking the picture.

Misha worked from morning until night. The performers and coaches changed, but Misha remained in the studio and rehearsed with each group of artists.

Tanya Koltsova, sensing how uncomfortable it was for Misha to see her in the studio, behaved capriciously. "Misha, may I leave rehearsal early today? I haven't been to the movies in a month." "Misha, I won't rehearse on point today because I am dancing *Chopiniana* this evening." During these rehearsals Yelena Kondratenko would lazily imitate Tanya. It was quite clear that she did not have the ability to dance the part. She was later excused from the rehearsals. Tanya continued to rehearse but because she was a *corps de ballet* dancer she did not really believe that she would actually dance Chloë. Only when it became clear that Kolpakova, who had never rehearsed, would not appear in *Daphnis and Chloë* did Tanya settle down and begin to work seriously. By that time it was already winter and very little time remained before the premiere.

FACING PAGE. *Baryshnikov in rehearsal.*

I think that Baryshnikov was right when he said to me that if he had remained in Leningrad, he would have made a ballerina out of Tanya. In terms of ballet art, Koltsova possessed a remarkably beautiful body with elongated proportions. She had a high jump in which she seemed weightless and had a beautiful line in her *arabesque*. But Misha was

speaking of a future he did not have. In truth, Tanya had no initiative, and not being spurred on to persistent work by anyone, she remained a dancer in the *corps de ballet*. She danced demi-solo roles for some time, but Misha's creative evening always remained the shining moment of her theatrical career.

When I went to a rehearsal of *The Prodigal Son,* Vazira Ganibalova was learning the part of the Siren. Ganibalova had graduated from the Uzbek Choreographic Institute in Tashkent and after that took Natalia Dudinskaya's *classe de perfectionnement* at the Leningrad ballet school. She had joined the Kirov at the same time as Misha. Ganibalova was a tall ballerina with a rather pretty oriental face and with very flexible legs and high extensions, but she was badly trained. She danced carelessly and appeared not to like to work. Her notion of herself as a ballerina was patently overblown. To make matters worse, Ganibalova had had a baby shortly before the rehearsals began and was not yet back in shape. She obviously needed to lose weight immediately. Once, when Misha was learning a high lift with her, my heart fluttered with fear. She drooped over him like a sack of flour and it seemed to me that she would crush him. Ganibalova regarded her work with overt disrespect. "No, no," she once said arrogantly to Mai Murdmaa, in my presence, "don't stage this movement for me because I won't do it anyway." The calm, polite, and slightly mocking Mai stepped aside and left Misha to negotiate with the capricious ballerina.

What a contrast Alla Osipenko's attitude toward her work presented with Ganibalova's behavior! Osipenko always stayed in shape and arrived at rehearsals ready to work. Osipenko was forty-one at the time but had no difficulties with this new choreography that she was unable to overcome. She was sixteen years older than Misha and yet they treated each other as equals, each acknowledging the other's talent and professionalism. Once, while working, they did not perform a lift properly. "Misha, excuse me, it's my fault," Alla apologized. Ganibalova continued to come to rehearsals for some time. If Murdmaa was working with Osipenko, she did not rehearse but stood by the wall and watched with a dissatisfied expression on her face. Later, she stopped coming altogether.

After the soloists went home or to other rehearsals, the work began with the *corps de ballet*. If the dancers were not on time, Misha would

FACING PAGE. *Tatyana Koltsova and Baryshnikov rehearsing in* Daphnis and Chloë.

155

Baryshnikov as Daphnis playing on a reed pipe.

actually go into the dressing rooms and round up those who were supposed to be at the rehearsal. Never hurrying, they would finally straggle into the studio.

Murdmaa began working with the *corps*. Her choreography was modern; the movements of the arms did not resemble the classical positions. The dancers, disregarding her directions, gave their wrists the customary

*Georgi Aleksidze rehearsing
with Irina Kolpakova for* Ballet
Divertissement *to Mozart's
music.*

roundedness. "But we weren't taught this way." The patient Mai would explain again.

Naturally, all the artists pulled themselves together as the premiere approached. Of course not everyone regarded the work so disparagingly. Irina Kolpakova, a thoroughly professional person, rehearsed very seriously. Misha himself worked with total commitment. He worried about himself, his colleagues, and about the impression Murdmaa's choreography would create. "Stop taking pictures and watch more carefully to see how all of this looks," he frequently said to me during the rehearsals. I photographed and watched. Misha put so much of his heart and his creative energy into this work that I received enormous pleasure simply as an observer.

I particularly remember a rehearsal of the beginning of *Daphnis and Chloë*. Daphnis played on an imaginary reed pipe. Murdmaa intentionally choreographed the role of Daphnis to include characteristics of Pan. With this motif, she emphasized the merging of the purity of Daphnis's soul with the purity of nature. It seemed as if nature itself was singing through the flute.

Toward the end of the rehearsal period, Misha began to invite ballet critics whose opinions he respected to watch.

In Russia, ballet critics are often the friends of choreographers and share the choreographers' point of view. Progressive critics are attempting, in conjunction with choreographers, to modernize productions by

157

TOP LEFT. *Alla Osipenko and Baryshnikov rehearsing the* pas de deux *of the Siren and the Son from* The Prodigal Son. *The critic Vera Krasovskaya is in the background by the mirror.*

TOP RIGHT, BOTTOM LEFT AND RIGHT. *Osipenko and Baryshnikov rehearsing the duet.*

supporting any fresh idea, any initiative of active ballet masters. Therefore, choreographers usually invite their critic friends to view the rehearsals in order to elicit any help they can offer.

And then it was time for the rehearsal onstage with an audience.

The first run-through. At this first rehearsal, there were also photographers in the audience. The official Kirov Theater photographer and the Vaganova Institute photographer were present. I had received permission to take pictures, at Baryshnikov's personal request. I was sitting there snapping away. Suddenly, during the intermission before *The Prodigal Son,* Pavel Kondratenko, Yelena Kondratenko's father, whom everyone in the theater believed to be a KGB worker, appeared in the aisle, impeccably and inconspicuously dressed as always. He approached me with an insidious and disagreeable expression on his face and said, "I forbid you to take photographs."

I began to protest. "How do you have the right to forbid me? Baryshnikov invited me."

"And who does Baryshnikov think he is?" Kondratenko replied.

It was senseless to argue with Kondratenko. I understood that but resisted anyway. I demanded that he explain the reason for the prohibition.

"Osipenko's costume is not ready yet. She will dance this performance in another costume."

"Why then am I not allowed to take pictures when the other photographers are?"

Kondratenko was tired of arguing with me. "The others are also forbidden," he declared and walked away. Then the other photographers were annoyed. They reproached me, and I asked for their pardon. What had I gained? Now everyone was forbidden to take photographs.

As later became clear, it was not just that Osipenko's costume was not ready. Someone in the artistic staff had demanded that her costume be replaced altogether; he apparently found it too revealing. Misha, however, refused to perform if Osipenko's costume was changed. The costume remained the way it had been conceived. (And all of us photographed her in this costume.) Misha won another victory, this time by taking advantage of the desperate position of the theater, just as he had overcome the foolishness and laziness of his ungrateful colleagues and the callous obtuseness of the administrators. But at what price? How many times did he swallow an undeserved insult in order to bring his creative evening to completion? Unfortunately, the annoyances and offenses did not end with the rehearsals.

FOLLOWING PAGES. TOP LEFT. *Baryshnikov and Vazira Ganibalova at rehearsal.* TOP RIGHT. *Baryshnikov rehearsing* The Prodigal Son. BOTTOM. *Rehearsal of* Daphnis and Chloë. *(Left to right) Tatyana Legat, Mai Murdmaa, Baryshnikov, and Tatyana Koltsova.* FULL PAGE. *After a rehearsal.*

159

THE END OF A BEAUTIFUL ERA

*Does my brain earn a slug, as a spot where an error occurred
earns a good pointing finger? Or should I hit
waterways, sort of like Christ?*

—Joseph Brodsky, "The End
of a Beautiful Era"

S lowly, the curtain goes up, revealing Daphnis seated alone on the edge of an empty stage, in a circle of light. He is sitting in an unconstrained, and, at the same time, an intentionally artistic ballet pose. Immersed in reverie, he is looking down at the floor. His pose is beautiful and manly; his body resembles the sculpture of a young Greek god. It is in this manner that the marble statues of the gods and heroes of antiquity gaze at their surroundings, in the cold quiet rooms of the Hermitage Museum on the banks of the Neva River.

Thus began the ballet *Daphnis and Chloë*. Baryshnikov, the god of dance, of breathtaking leaps and turns, was sitting motionless on the stage. The auditorium was silent, with the stillness that arises from the genuine contact of an artist with his audience. It is difficult to hold such a pause at the beginning of a ballet, before the viewer has been drawn into the action, before his imagination has been stirred. And this pause, this silence, began an entire evening, with latecomers still getting to

163

their seats, with the audience not yet prepared for anything and not yet believing anything. Yet all the same, silence prevailed. The audience was trying to understand: what is the motionless dancer, seated by the edge of the stage in a circle of light, thinking about in his public solitude? The ability to sustain such a pause reveals a high degree of theatrical mastery; it is the ineffable magic of the theater.

Slowly, rising from the floor, Baryshnikov began to come to life. His first solo dance consisted of beautiful, sculptural poses, several of which recalled the god Pan as he is often portrayed in paintings. During this scene, Daphnis was playing on an imaginary instrument, Pan's reed pipe. The son of Hermes and a nymph, Daphnis was a shepherd and a poet and a musician. The great Pan himself, god of the forest, god of nature, taught Daphnis to play. Pan had carved his pipe from the reed that the nymph Syrinx had turned herself into in order to escape from Pan when he was pursuing her.

The ballet *Daphnis and Chloë* was first created by Mikhail Fokine in 1912 in Paris for Diaghilev's *Ballets Russes*. Ravel composed the music especially for Fokine, whose libretto was an adaptation of the story of Longus, a bard of ancient Greece. Murdmaa abridged Fokine's libretto. The outline of the story remained: brigands imperil the idyllic love of the shepherd Daphnis and the shepherdess Chloë. Bryaxis the pirate abducts Chloë, but the nymphs rescue her and return her to Daphnis. However, the minute details of Fokine's ballet and the quantity of secondary plot lines were unsuitable for the contemporary nature of Murdmaa's choreography. Not only were the shepherds and shepherdesses, including the old shepherd Lammon who told the story of Syrinx and Pan, absent from this version of the ballet, but even Pan himself was missing. Nevertheless, Murdmaa retained the images of Pan and Syrinx in the ballet, intertwining their story with the story of Daphnis and Chloë by means of purely visual associations. Moreover, Murdmaa constructed Daphnis and Chloë's first *pas de deux* with light, beautiful jumps and fleeting contact between the lovers in the lifts—a duet meant to evoke the image of Pan's pursuit of Syrinx more than the idyllic love of Daphnis and Chloë. Koltsova's beautiful, long-legged, cool Chloë was in fact more like a nymph than a shepherdess. All of the love and tenderness emanated from Baryshnikov's Daphnis. It was he who pursued Chloë;

FACING PAGE. *The beginning of* Daphnis and Chloë.

164

ABOVE, RIGHT, AND FACING
PAGE. *Daphnis.*

166

he was captivated by her, but she evaded him. In her attraction to Daphnis's playing on the reed pipe, and in her movements in the air with him, she shared love with Daphnis, as if against her will. This disparity of feelings added a somewhat disquieting nuance to the idyll.

Daphnis had many beautiful leaps in this first duet, and Baryshnikov was flying. It was not simply that he was overcoming gravity. He was flying, as birds do. It seemed that he was created to fly.

During the middle of the ballet the intrigue unfolds. Bryaxis abducts Chloë and the nymphs intervene to rescue her and return her to Daphnis.

The separation revealed to the lovers the seriousness of their feelings for one another. The last *pas de deux* was a duet of mutual love—although, as before, Daphnis's feelings dominated. This last scene consisted of uninterrupted movement. The dancers were two bounding brooks that would merge, finally, into one stream with a slower course. The lyrical action, the tender, chaste games of two grown-up children, and the games transformed into a whisper of love were the impressions that remained with me from this ballet. Misha was a young half-god, half-boy, and a poet in this aesthetic ballet, composing songs for his empty-headed girl friend, his evasive muse. Murdmaa gradually moved her heroes farther and farther upstage from the light. The ballet ended with a tender kiss of the lovers, already almost indistinguishable in the penumbral twilight.

Ballet Divertissement to Mozart's music was presented in the second act of the evening. The choreographer, Gogi Aleksidze, had a talent for creating plotless ballets where the choreography was a reflection of each musical phrase. This work was based on classical dance; Aleksidze styled the ballet in a traditional manner. Baryshnikov's partner, Irina Kolpakova, danced her part irreproachably. This was not the first time Kolpakova had appeared in one of Aleksidze's ballets, and she danced with great artistic sensitivity. The true focus of the ballet was the male variation, danced brilliantly by Misha, and which always provoked a storm of applause. In every second of his presence onstage, in every jump and movement, Misha conveyed the style of old-fashioned refinement tinged with a slight irony toward this refinement.

The evening ended with Murdmaa's philosophical ballet *The Prodigal*

TOP, MIDDLE, AND BOTTOM.
*Chloë: Tatyana Koltsova;
Daphnis: Baryshnikov.*

FACING PAGE, TOP. *Daphnis
playing on Pan's reed pipe.*
FACING PAGE, BOTTOM, AND
FOLLOWING PAGES. *Chloë:
Koltsova; Daphnis:
Baryshnikov.*

171

Son, to Sergei Prokofiev's music. Baryshnikov's appearance in the role of the Son was to be perhaps his most serious work in Leningrad. The period of intuitive discoveries had ended. A master appeared on the stage: the artist Baryshnikov, working consciously and with inspiration. The era of his creative flourishing had begun.

Murdmaa's version of *The Prodigal Son* has little in common with George Balanchine's famous ballet. Murdmaa used the old scenario of Boris Kochno, but in other respects this was an entirely original work of art. Murdmaa and Baryshnikov both saw the work as a contemporary, symbolic interpretation of the biblical parable.

The Son leaves his home, a world of stifling love, not because the temptations of the outside world attract him, but to break away from the protective arms of his mother, father, and sisters, as all children reaching adulthood everywhere must. Beyond the walls of home, adult life, filled with alluring secrets, beckoned. Only the collision of the innocent Son's heart with real life—and the result of this collision—had significance.

The Son breaks free from his home and remains alone on the empty stage in the spotlight. Delighting in his freedom, he exults. And then the Siren enters the spotlight.

Alla Osipenko's entrance was unhurried, as if from nowhere. Her amazing figure was tautly covered in dark leotards. The Siren looks totally different from any woman the Son has seen before. And he loses his head. The *pas de deux* was closer to a duel than a duet—with Alla Osipenko perfect both as a ballerina and as an actress. For the Son, the meeting with the Siren is the first confrontation with the world of adults, a world whose internal contradictions he does not understand. In particular, he does not understand deception. For him, sensual attraction is identical to real love. Woman is an enigma to him. She is potent, majestic, and infernal at one and the same time. Incomprehensibly, she teaches him love and yet does not love him herself. The invariable half-smile on her lips seems to the Son to be the sign of a secret link to him—but he cannot perceive its significance. This spiritual elusiveness (a quality, to some degree, in all of Osipenko's heroines) tormented, attracted, infuriated, and gave delight.

Later, some companions appear—boys, just like the Son; his peers. The dancers were dressed in identical practice clothes, as if in uniform.

The Son is still filled with the ideals of his home. When the boys vow friendship, he believes them. Rapturously, he copies their jumps and their awkward, modern, teenage dancing, not noticing their mockery of him. The Son is happy: he had been seeking the friendship of peers and now he has found it. Suddenly, without any transition, the collapse of childish illusions begins. The companions have played with the naïve Son out of boredom and idleness. Now they begin to taunt and torment him. With the same smiles on their faces with which they had just lured the Son into friendship, the companions hurl him from side to side, jeering at and hitting him. The Son flings himself on the Siren, but she sides with the other boys, and does not stand up for the Son, participating in the cruel game on the side of the youths. Again and again the Son throws himself on her with the obstinacy of desperation. He tries with all his might to seize her from the companions and to compel her to love him, to force her to be the way she had seemed to him at the beginning.

Eventually, bored with the game, the companions run off. The Siren remains. The Son, crushed, crawls along the stage toward her, desperately hoping to catch and keep her. But the Siren no longer sees the Son. Beautiful, cold, and mysterious, with the same unwavering smile on her lips, she leaves the stage, slowly stepping over the body of the Son with her long legs. She has come from nowhere and she disappears into nowhere.

Abandoned by the Siren, the Son returns home, crawling, rolling, and running. In his blind despair, he seeks the place where there were people who loved him. When he returns home, his Father takes the Son into his arms and pardons him, as in the biblical parable. But the ballet does not end with the scene of forgiveness, because the theme of the modern ballet was not disobedience and forgiveness. The moral problem was only whether the Son endured the trial by evil or if it had killed his soul.

The same group of participants as in the beginning—the Father, Mother, the two Sisters, and the Son—gradually become submerged in darkness. The spotlight in which they stand tapers, and the darkness surrounds them more and more densely. But now the family does not hold the Son by the hand as in the beginning of the ballet. Now they

ABOVE AND LEFT. *Kolpakova
and Baryshnikov dancing in
Ballet Divertissement.*

175

seek shelter behind his back, and he stands, with his arms spread, protecting his family from the approaching darkness. The Son is no longer the delicate child who had run away from home. But the collision with the world has not broken him. He understands that ignorance of evil does not save one from evil. He has returned home as a man, a protector of the good and the defenseless. He peers tensely into the approaching, thickening dark, leaving us, as if it were the last frame of a film, with the image of the watchful but calm face of the Son.

The secret of Baryshnikov's artistic genius and of the special love that was felt for him in Russia emerged in this creative evening. It was not only a matter of his talent, although that was part of it. But in developing the interpretation of a role, Baryshnikov expressed the moral ideals of his time. He was as much a voice of his time as Ulanova had been of hers. He asserted that evil does not destroy the moral foundations of modern man; that in the soulless, terrifying world of contemporary Russia, the concept of spiritual purity still exists; that not only individual sacrifice for the sake of saving one's own soul was possible, but also the

178

confrontation of evil for the sake of defending others. He was one of the chosen about whom Peter Brook wrote in *The Empty Space,* "If he [the artist] is relaxed, open, and attuned, then the invisible will take possession of him; through him, it will reach us." Part of the public's love for Baryshnikov was an unconscious gratitude to him for revealing to us the lofty ideal of a contemporary hero.

With *The Prodigal Son,* Baryshnikov attained the creative summit of his Leningrad career. Applause and cries of "Ba-ry-shni-kov! Bravo!" thundered out. Baskets of flowers and bouquets filled his dressing room and apartment.

The *artsoviet* met after the preview. Misha called me afterward, speaking in a completely dead voice. Many members of the *artsoviet* had panned Misha's creative evening. Leonid Yakobson believed that, after Balanchine, no one had the right to stage *The Prodigal Son.* Yakobson's point of view was based on his artistic outlook. The other negative opinions were simply spiteful grumbling about modern choreography and resentment of another's success and courage in trying new ideas. Misha

179

ABOVE, RIGHT, AND
FOLLOWING PAGES. *The Siren:*
Alla Osipenko;
the Son: Baryshnikov.

The work with which he had been occupied for half a year and on which he had placed such hopes had brought him only bitterness. The indefatigable Suslik, who at this time literally never left Misha alone, continually accompanied him to various parties, where they drank. Once, after one of Baryshnikov's performances, a group of us went to visit the poet to celebrate his birthday. Misha was both tired and sad. Suslik sat next to him at the table and the following dialogue took place.

"Misha, drink!"

"I don't want to."

"Misha drink! Misha drink! Misha drink!"

I asked Suslik much later, after Misha had gone forever, "Why did you make him drink?"

He answered, "I saw that he felt bad and thought if he drank he would feel better." Perhaps Suslik really thought so.

Later on that evening, Misha actually cheered up somehow. He even imitated a plain, Russian fellow and danced. But his whole life by then was a kind of senseless self-immolation. There was nothing for him to look forward to. Finally, in May, the premiere of Igor Belsky's new ballet, 183

Icarus, took place. I did not go to the preview. Misha attended and called me afterward; in a hopeless tone of voice he said, "Don't go. The ballet is terrible." The hopes he had pinned on Belsky had collapsed. Only *Komsomol* congresses, drinking binges, and Suslik remained.

It was impossible at that time to say anything to Misha concerning his life-style or even Suslik. He would lose his temper and raise his voice, as if his freedom were being infringed. The worse off he was, the angrier he became with those who tried to help him, no doubt because no one truly could help him. I did not try to tempt fate any further and occupied myself with my own affairs. Even Slava, Misha's most patient friend, gave up.

Misha was preparing to dance Prince Siegfried in *Swan Lake* at the Kirov the following season. He demonstrated some passages at my house, between the table and the bookshelf, and he described his future Siegfried to me. Siegfried would not be deceived at the ball and would not mistake the Black Swan for Odette but simply and frankly would become captivated by another woman. Once again responsibility for one's own actions, unmitigated by any extenuating circumstances, would have been the theme. Unfortunately, Baryshnikov did not dance *Swan Lake* at the Kirov Theater. I finally saw a standard interpretation of Siegfried by Baryshnikov onstage at the Metropolitan Opera.

On April 30, 1974, Baryshnikov danced *Giselle* at the Kirov Theater with Natalia Bessmertnova. The house was packed, as always with Baryshnikov's performances, and even more so that evening because of Bessmertnova. All of the balletomanes, all of the friends, the critics from Leningrad and Moscow, and the actors from the dramatic theaters attended—in short, everyone who was able to obtain a ticket was at the performance. This was a real ballet celebration, and proved to be Baryshnikov's last performance in Russia.

By May, it seemed that Misha was beginning to return to normal. In any case, he began to go out without Suslik. He began to ask questions again about the lives of his friends. Negotiations were being conducted to make a television production in Leningrad of Grigorovich's *The Nutcracker* with Baryshnikov and Bessmertnova in the leading roles. Misha loved this ballet. At that time, he and I even discussed his joining the Bolshoi Ballet in Moscow if the situation at the Kirov remained as hope-

less as it had been up until then. We talked about this in May when he came to visit me. Misha was quiet and downcast. We also spoke of his relationship with Tanya and whether or not they should live together again. Occupied with my own personal life and the doleful problems of a secret and unrequited love for another man, I made what I thought was an intelligent remark about the importance of inspiring love in others, as I went into the kitchen to make some coffee. When I returned, Misha was sitting at the piano trying to recall a forgotten piece of music. I put his cup of coffee on the piano but he did not look up. This was the last time that Misha visited me at my home on the Petrograd Side.

Later, in a conversation in New York, Misha said to me, as if in response to my remark, "Does one really live in order to be necessary to someone?"

187

TOP, MIDDLE, BOTTOM, AND
FACING PAGE. *The Son meets
the companions.*

At the end of May, Misha left with the troupe of ballet artists from the Moscow and Leningrad companies for Canada and South America. The group was scheduled to fly to Toronto from Moscow in the beginning of June; therefore, Misha had to leave for the capital. On the evening before his departure, Misha picked me up in his car and we set out with Slava Santnaneev and Valya, his oldest friend, who was practically a sister to him. We went to the home of the small woman with the low voice whom I had first met on the corner in front of her home, when she held a package of coffee and stood next to a happy, gray-eyed boy. Now this boy, with a gaunt and tired face, and the three of us, all in despondent moods, came to see her and sit for a while before Baryshnikov's departure on tour. I had no presentiment, no idea that we were saying good-bye to Misha for the last time. We had always gathered together, in a larger or smaller group, every time Misha had gone abroad. I remember well how, on another occasion, we had seen him off to Spain. Misha was still living in his second apartment then. He was in very good spirits and got extremely drunk. Slava, as an older friend, and Tanya, as his wife, got angry with us, the guests, thinking that we had encouraged him to get drunk. But Misha himself was very cheerful and full of laughter; he escorted his guests to the stairs and continued to yell after us as we descended.

Now, we sat at the table silently. It is possible that each of us had our own reason for feeling low; it is also possible that Misha's mental condition was communicated to us. Of all of us, only the young woman with the low voice spoke. She did not know how to react to this situation and made some rather poor jokes. Misha greeted her jokes, which did not seem funny at all, with forced laughter. We sat, saw Misha off, and then went home. Tanya Koltsova later told me that Misha called her before leaving for Moscow and talked with her for a long time. She was sitting on the floor in the corridor where the telephone hung. Misha would not let her go, repeating, "Don't hang up. Talk with me a little more." The last of his Leningrad friends with whom Misha spoke before his departure was apparently Suslik, who claimed that Misha called him from Moscow just before his flight.

Then Misha flew to the West—as it turned out—forever.

Baryshnikov, the Son.

The Son.

FACING PAGE, TOP. *The Son tries to keep the Siren from leaving.* BOTTOM. *The Son's despair.*

193

FACING PAGE. *The final scene of* The Prodigal Son. TOP. *Baryshnikov taking a curtain call at the premiere in response to the applause.* BOTTOM. *Backstage after the premiere; from left to right: Baryshnikov, Igor Belsky, the artistic director of the Kirov Ballet, and Pavel Kondratenko, the administrator.*

195

Baryshnikov and Foma. 1974.

FACING PAGE. *Baryshnikov's
last performance in Russia:
Giselle. Giselle: Natalia
Bessmertnova.*

I N T E R V I E W

The following interview with Mikhail Baryshnikov, entitled "The Creation of an Image: Our Interlocutor—Honored Artist of RSFSR Mikhail Baryshnikov," conducted by Arsen Degen, appeared in Smena, *a Leningrad newspaper, on December 8, 1973.*

H is dancing is an absorbing, intensive pursuit for the elusive beauty of art, the endless aspiration toward an ideal." Thus wrote one perspicacious critic about the then very young artist and *Komsomolets* Mikhail Baryshnikov. The brilliant, masterly, cheerful dancing of this talented youth is familiar to admirers of the ballet far beyond Leningrad. In his twenty-five years, he has succeeded in many ways, creating outstanding roles in performances at the Kirov Theater of Opera and Ballet. He has also received a series of major awards: gold medals at the ballet competitions in Varna and Moscow and the Vaslav Nijinsky Prize of Paris. A great number of friends call him Misha, but Mikhail Nikolaevich is a member of the artistic council of the theater and he has just had conferred upon him the title of Honored Artist of the Republic.*

As is known, you were born and began to study choreography in Riga. How did you end up in Leningrad's Vaganova Choreographic Institute?

---

*Honored Artist of the Russian Soviet Federal Socialist Republic (RSFSR). There are fifteen republics in the Soviet Union.

In 1964 the Theater of Opera and Ballet of the Latvian SSR [Soviet Socialist Republic] went on tour to Leningrad and brought with it a group of pupils. We took part in mime and dance scenes. As soon as I found myself in Leningrad, I fell in love with this beautiful city. I came to try my luck at the Vaganova Institute and was placed in the seventh* class of the wonderful teacher, Aleksandr Ivanovich Pushkin, with whom I studied for all three school years.

Won't you tell us what this professor of male dancing meant to you?

For me, Aleksandr Ivanovich is the standard of professionalism. Teachers have differing styles: some are kind, almost hail-fellow-well-met with the pupils; others are disciplinary. Pushkin was the golden mean. During the lessons, Pushkin did not employ ostentatious means or effects. He was reserved, firm, with the pupils. People in his classes for the first time often wondered, "What is so special here?" Everything, as it were, would turn out by itself. Of course, he had his system of teaching, but this is a special question. Primarily, he had real inter-relationships with his pupils. Patiently, without pressure, he led the student to the idea of self-education. Everyone educated himself—under his [Pushkin's] guidance, of course. This helped us in later, independent work. Our mentor taught professionalism on a large scale.

In 1969 you received the gold medal of the first ballet competition in Moscow. What did the competition give to you in terms of creativity?

It was a wonderful opportunity for me that the theater management invited Leonid Veniaminovich Yakobson to stage the contemporary short ballet required for the competition, because he is famous for working in this genre. His proposal to create *Vestris,* a ballet that evokes the legendary dancer of the same name, surprised me. But, from the first re-hearsals, everything went very well. There was little time left before the competition, but when Yakobson wants something, he manages it. For any dancer or ballerina, a meeting with Leonid Veniaminovich is an event to be remembered for the rest of his or her life. You know, he does not simply stage a concert number; he stages it with the individuality of the

---

*Elementary and high school education in the Soviet Union is divided into ten grades. Pupils begin at age seven and graduate at seventeen or eighteen.

artist in mind. I trust Yakobson's taste unconditionally. Choreographically, he revealed qualities in my dancing that I never knew I had.

During six years of work in the Kirov Theater, you have created a number of roles in productions of the classical and contemporary repertory. Which of these have become landmarks in your career?

Probably Adam in Andrey Petrov's ballet *The Creation of the World.* You see, this was not a debut in an already finished ballet but my first serious work on a new production—"live" with the choreographers. At first I was afraid; my limited experience with the eurhythmic material that the ballet masters, Natalia Kasatkina and Vladimir Vasiliev, required frightened me. I did not dance naturally. It seems to me that I had not completely assimilated the role, even by the premiere. Much of it was created later; with each performance, the image changed. It was hard to give a believable and smooth transition from Adam-child to the tragic quality of the last act. It is interesting for me to dance this ballet, but difficult. Each performance is created as if anew. Its movement is now organic for me.

And after that was Albrecht in *Giselle.*

In connection with the role of Albrecht, I wanted to ask you one more question. How do you see your interpretation of the classical ballet? Do you consider all the traditions of the role you are dancing and of the production as a whole, or do you try to approach both with a fresh view?

Knowing this production and knowing many of its interpreters, I did not especially try to dispense with what had been. But every artist ought to know his own individuality and should attempt, either in his head or on paper, to adapt the choreographic form and movements to one's individual qualities. I had always wanted to dance in *Giselle*, but for a long time I could not decide even mentally how to put myself in the part of Albrecht. The already developed representation impeded me. I wouldn't have been able simply to repeat Sergeyev, Kuznetsov, or Vikulov. It seemed to me that I would have looked absurd in their image and even in their costume. The first act in particular troubled me. I did not see myself as a fop or seducer. To be slightly in love, to be carried away in order to repent later? Then, suddenly, the solution and the resolution came to me: Albrecht cannot not be sincere in his feeling toward Giselle. I saw no other approach for myself. The apparent sudden shift between the acts is, in my opinion, only external—a primordially evil man cannot truly be reborn. The theme is not so much a clash with social prejudices as a moral responsibility for one's own love.

The Polish director Adam Hanuszkiewicz once said that *Hamlet* should be staged every three to four years, because time puts an imprint on the performers. I think that the same thing occurs with *Giselle*.

You have participated in the Leningrad Ballet's tours to England, Japan, Spain, and Australia and have recently returned from Bulgaria. What were the most striking artistic impressions for you?

In Spain, the flamenco in Barcelona. I had seen this dance earlier, when Spanish dance groups came to Leningrad. But in Barcelona the entire atmosphere of a long performance on a small stage in a small, semi-dark restaurant struck me—dancing, interludes of guitar playing, and then dancing again. Much more about Spanish dancing became clear to me. I hope to employ this feeling in some sort of new work.

And then, Japan. It is impossible not to fall in love with that country. Its extraordinary mysteriousness, even a mythological quality, is enrapturing. The choreographer Gogi Aleksidze is planning to stage a ballet on a Japanese theme in which the traditions of Kabuki theater would be refracted in modern eurhythmics. I hope to participate in this work.

You began to speak about the future. If you don't object, continue on this subject. The preparation for your creative evening, which is planned for the beginning of 1974, is now going on. What do you intend to include in its program? What guided you in your choice?

The simplest thing would have been to dance an act from *Don Quixote* or "The Shades" from *La Bayadère*. However, I wanted something new. Right now, it is still hard to say what specifically I will manage to prepare. Things are getting more definite—rehearsals have begun—with two one-act ballets: *The Prodigal Son* by Sergei Prokofiev and *Daphnis and Chloë* by Maurice Ravel. Both were created by Mai Murdmaa, the ballet master in Tallin, and are being transferred to our theater with changes to suit the new interpreters. Why did I propose these works? In the first place, the music is beautiful. Second, Mai Murdmaa, in my opinion, is one of the few ballet mistresses who successfully resolves a ballet with purely choreographic means. Mai is a person and an artist of great integrity; in her productions there are no wasted movements, and because of this there is an abundance of fantasy and imagery. The hero of *The Prodigal Son* is not a concrete person but a symbol. There is no space for imagery; analysis, self-analysis, and generalization are demanded. I have not yet had the chance to dance a role like that. It is complicated and interesting.

What new roles in the basic repertory of the theater are you preparing? What do you dream about?

I am thinking about many roles. In the very near future I hope to mature into the roles of Ferkhad in *The Legend of Love* and Danila in *The Stone Flower*. I dream about Yury Nikolaevich Grigorovich's production of *The Nutcracker*.

What is dear to you, apart from the stage?

Friends and Foma. [The huge, white, shaggy poodle, Foma, who was listening to our conversation, good-naturedly barked.] I love music. Particularly Rachmaninov. I collect the records of the French *chansonniers*: Barbara, Brel, Brassens, Aznavour. . . .

203

I know that you frequently, and with interest, attend performances at the dramatic theaters. What are your preferences here?

I love to see productions with well-defined directing and I delight in outstanding acting, such as Volkov and Durov in Anatoly Efros's production of *Don Juan*, Yakovlev in *Romeo and Juliet*. From among Leningrad actors, there are Yursky and Basilashvili in *Molière*, Osobik in *Tsar Fedor Ioannovich*.

In ending our discussion, I would like to ask: What question would you ask yourself if you were in my position?

What do you want?

Splendid. Now, please, answer.

No. Now, please, you answer for me and I will listen and, if necessary, I will correct you.

I want several productions to be staged each season in my dear and beloved theater, in which there would be new, diverse, and interesting roles for me. Also, that there would not be enforced idleness, creatively speaking, that it would not be necessary to seek ballet masters oneself. In short, let there be much more serious, absorbing work.

A P P E N D I X

R O L E S   A N D   F I R S T
A P P E A R A N C E S

1. Graduation Performance from the Vaganova Choreographic Institute. *Pas de deux* from *Don Quixote* (Ludwig Minkus/Marius Petipa), with Ella Kubatova. June 8, 13, 16, 1967.

2. *Spanish Miniatures* (to folk music/Jerardo Viana Gomez de Fonsea). "Good," a solo. 1967.

3. Yakobson's Choreographic Miniatures. *Eternal Spring* (Claude Debussy/Leonid Yakobson), with Yelena Yevteyeva. During 1967–1968 season.

4. *Goryanka* (Kazhlayev/Oleg Vinogradov). The Friend of Asiat: Baryshnikov; Asiat: Ella Komleva. March 16, 1968.

5. *Swan Lake* (Petr Tchaikovsky/Lev Ivanov, Petipa). Friend of Prince Siegfried: Baryshnikov. *Pas de trois* with Yelena Yevteyeva and Ksenia Ter-Stepanova. August 18, 1968.

6. *Chopiniana* (Frédéric Chopin/Jules Perrot, Petipa). The Youth: Baryshnikov; with Alla Sizova. March 30, 1969.

7. *Giselle* (Adolph Adam/Perrot, Petipa). *Pas de deux* with Olga Vtorushina. April–May 1969.

8. *Vestris* (Gennady Banshchikov/Leonid Yakobson). Vestris: Baryshnikov. June 1969.

9. *Don Quixote*. Basil: Baryshnikov; Kitri: Ninel Kurgapkina. November 10, 1969.

10. *Romeo and Juliet* (Hector Berlioz/Igor Chernyshev). Romeo: Vadim Gulyaev; Juliet: Irina Kolpakova; Mercutio: Baryshnikov. The creative evening of Irina Kolpakova. December 28, 1969.

11. *The Crystal Palace* (*Symphony in C*, Georges Bizet/George Balanchine). Concert performance with Natalia Makarova. May 8, 1970.

12. *The Sleeping Beauty* (Tchaikovsky/Petipa). Prince Désiré: Baryshnikov; Aurora: Alla Sizova. June 21, 1970.

13. *Hamlet* (Nikolai Chervinsky/Konstantin Sergeyev). Hamlet: Baryshnikov; Ophelia: Yelena Yevteyeva. Preview: December 10, 1970. Premiere: December 30, 1970.

14. *The Creation of the World* (Andrey Petrov/Natalia Kasatkina, Vladimir Vasiliev). Adam: Baryshnikov; Eve: Irina Kolpakova. Preview: March 20, 1971. Premiere: March 23, 1971.

15. Concert in honor of the eighty-fifth birthday of Fedor Lopukhov (in the October Concert Hall). *The Ice Maiden* (Edvard Grieg/Lopukhov). The Dance of the Bird: Baryshnikov. December 20, 1971.

16. *Giselle*. Albrecht: Baryshnikov; Giselle: Alla Sizova. January 5, 1972.

17. *The Prince of the Pagodas* (Benjamin Britten/Vinogradov). Prince Salamander: Baryshnikov; Princess Rose: Alla Sizova. December 30, 1972.

18. *Le Corsaire* (Adam/Petipa). Conrad: Baryshnikov. July 5, 1973.

19. Baryshnikov's creative evening. *Daphnis and Chloë* (Maurice Ravel/Mai Murdmaa). Daphnis: Baryshnikov; Chloë: Tatyana Koltsova. *Ballet Divertissement* (W. A. Mozart/Georgi Aleksidze). Baryshnikov and Irina Kolpakova. Natalia Bolshakova, the female soloist in the second cast, danced in the second premiere. *The Prodigal Son* (Sergei Prokofiev/Mai

Murdmaa). The Son: Baryshnikov; the Siren: Alla Osipenko. Previews: February 15–19, 1974. Premieres: February 21, 24, 1974.

20. Baryshnikov's last performance in Russia was in *Giselle* with Natalia Bessmertnova on April 30, 1974.

T E L E V I S I O N A P P E A R A N C E S

1. *The Tale of Nikishka the Serf* (a ballet made for television by Kiril Laskari). Nikishka: Baryshnikov; the Bird of Harmony: Yelena Yevteyeva. 1968.

2. *Fiesta* (based on *The Sun Also Rises* by Ernest Hemingway; directed by Sergei Yursky). Pedro Romero: Baryshnikov. Spring 1971.

3. *Pas de deux* from *Don Quixote*. With Svetlana Yefremova. End of 1972–beginning of 1973.

4. *Adagio* from *Giselle*. With Natalia Bessmertnova. Winter 1972.

5. *Adagio* from *The Sleeping Beauty*. With Irina Kolpakova. 1973.

6. *Adagio* from *Swan Lake*, Act II. With Lyudmilla Putinova. 1973.

P R I Z E S

International Ballet Competition in Varna, Bulgaria, 1967. Gold medal. *Pas de deux* from *Le Corsaire, Coppélia,* and *The Flames of Paris,* with Olga Vtorushina.

International Ballet Competition in Moscow, June 1969. Gold medal. *Vestris* (Gennady Banshchikov/Leonid Yakobson). Variations from *La Bayadère* and *Paquita.*

Nijinsky Prize of Paris, 1969.

INDEX

Note: Page numbers in boldface refer to photographs.

210